PSYCHOLOGY LIBRARY EDITIONS: HISTORY OF PSYCHOLOGY

Volume 2

TEMPERAMENT

TEMPERAMENT
A Survey of Psychological Theories

CONSTANCE BLOOR

Routledge
Taylor & Francis Group

LONDON AND NEW YORK

First published in 1928 by Methuen & Co. Ltd

This edition first published in 2020
by Routledge
2 Park Square, Milton Park, Abingdon, Oxon OX14 4RN

and by Routledge
52 Vanderbilt Avenue, New York, NY 10017

Routledge is an imprint of the Taylor & Francis Group, an informa business

British Library Cataloguing in Publication Data
A catalogue record for this book is available from the British Library

ISBN: 978-0-367-40845-9 (Set)
ISBN: 978-1-00-301614-4 (Set) (ebk)
ISBN: 978-0-367-41847-2 (Volume 2) (hbk)
ISBN: 978-0-367-41851-9 (Volume 2) (pbk)
ISBN: 978-0-367-81653-7 (Volume 2) (ebk)

Publisher's Note
The publisher has gone to great lengths to ensure the quality of this reprint but points out that some imperfections in the original copies may be apparent.

Disclaimer
The publisher has made every effort to trace copyright holders and would welcome correspondence from those they have been unable to trace.

TEMPERAMENT
A SURVEY OF PSYCHOLOGICAL THEORIES

BY

CONSTANCE BLOOR, M.A.
LECTURER IN EDUCATION AT THE STOCKWELL TRAINING COLLEGE

METHUEN & CO. LTD.
36 ESSEX STREET W.C.
LONDON

First Published in 1928

CONTENTS

CHAPTER I

INTRODUCTION

THE assertion is often made that the Psychology of to-day tends to emphasize the individual and his differences rather than the universal and alike. In adopting an attitude of experimental detachment Psychologists would appear to be approaching more nearly to the methods of Biology and even to those of the physical sciences. It is possibly true that along these lines only can the claims of Psychology to recognition as an exact science be established. If, in the laboratory, the psychologist can measure and correlate, and devise a law which will fit the measurements, and on the basis of which further predictions can be made, then he will receive at the hands of scientists the recognition of equality. Until that time he is apt to be looked upon with suspicion by the chemists and physicists as one who seeks on the one hand to ally himself with pure speculative philosophy, and on the other to claim for his subject a position among the exact sciences.

It may be useful to inquire initially into the nature of the criticisms levelled at Psychology by scientific critics. These criticisms appear in general to be directed against the looseness of the terms employed and against the introduction of too many speculative hypotheses. The critics also inquire with

reference to the measurements of Psychology—
'What are the the units of measurement which
you employ and to what extent are they invariable?'
An example may be quoted in reference to the
concept of energy, in terms of which many psychologists find it convenient to state the problems of
mental behaviour. In the science of Mathematical
Physics the term 'energy' has a very definite and
circumscribed meaning and unit of measurement.
The psychologist may reply that it is open to him,
also, taking the dictionary definition of energy, to
employ this term for his purposes, but he lays
himself open to the retort that by the mere adoption
of a term he does not in any way further the scientific
progress of his subject. Methods of science demand
that the terms used should be in accordance with
the nature of the material investigated. Having
analysed the material at his disposal the scientist
must then find a term to fit the facts, and should
the term so chosen be already in the dictionary he
is yet free to circumscribe its meaning in reference
to his particular line of investigation. The argument
would appear to be that in the carrying over of
terms from common usage or from other fields of
inquiry into a science, which may from the nature of
its material require a different nomenclature, there is
a danger of transferring with it irrelevant associations.

The question as to how far the conceptions and
phraseology of the physical sciences will prove
inadequate for the needs of Psychology is a difficult one. In the introductory chapter to his study
of Experimental Psychology, Myers states the
problem thus : ' We are now in a position to realize

that it is only the possibility of giving a physical expression to mental states, which confers on Psychology the rank of a science.'[1] But this statement must be regarded as qualified by a previous one. 'We must regard experimental psychology as but one mode of studying psychological problems, not all of which however, can be approached from the side of experiment. Far from being independent, experimental psychology has arisen as a refinement of general psychology.'[2]

It is the existence of this supposed 'general psychology' which appears to constitute a real difficulty to many inquirers. It is interesting to contrast for example the criticisms outlined above which issue from the biologist and to a still greater extent from the physicist with those levelled from within the ranks of the psychologists by those who devote themselves principally to the particular province of Psychotherapy. One hears frequently from this source the admission that the psychoanalyst can find little of interest or usefulness in what he in general refers to as the 'academic psychology.' At this stage of psychological progress it would probably be unjust to suppose that the stigma of 'academic' denotes in the mind of the critic a belief that such psychology emanates purely from speculative thought. It is perhaps more likely to mean that it appears to him to have little connexion with the more urgent problem of maladjustment to the conditions of life, with which he himself is so usefully employed. The apparent

---

[1] C. S. Myers. Experimental Psychology. Ch. I. page 4.
[2] Myers. Experimental Psychology. Ch. I. page 1.

divorce in sympathy between the different schools, resulting as it must in a disastrous lack of cohesion in the subject itself would seem to indicate a difference in emphasis in the line of approach. Those who, with the Psycho-Analytic school concentrate upon the life and conflict of the individual, consider him as a reacting whole, an essentially autonomous creature. To deal with him as such would imply a danger of submergence in the vast complexity of the problem which can only be avoided by a deliberate simplification. Such a simplification would find a parallel in other fields of scientific work, and is, in itself, a legitimate procedure. Psycho-Analysis might not unduly claim that, while it has reduced the problem to a few broad generalizations, there is, in the technique elaborated for dealing with them, a delicate complexity which is able to meet the demands of widely differing individuals. If the hypothesis adopted by this school of thought may appear to be in the nature of speculation, its exponents can at least point to its consistency with experimental testing.

On the other hand, apparently remote from this line of approach is the work of those psychologists, who with infinite precautions are engaged in the laboratory exploration of such discrete cognitive processes as 'imagery' and 'attention' and those who, nearer perhaps to the situations of life are investigating differences in intelligence and in specific abilities. Their method might be briefly described as the elimination of those factors which are irrelevant to the investigation of the moment, and the criticism which is often brought against them, is, that they eliminate life itself. They may claim with justice, that only so can quantitative accuracy be secured, and that the results so obtained can in virtue of their reliability, find a surer application in the situations of life.

The question which arises is—' Assuming that such experiments are carried to the furthest degree of accuracy and extent, will it be possible so to weave together the results that they may form a complete science of human behaviour, or will it remain true that ' the whole is greater than the sum of the parts ? '

If the linking up of such results would constitute a complete explanation then behaviour would be determinate. There is, for example, the effort which is being made to establish a correlation more or less perfect between quantitative factors in behaviour and physiological reactions. Assuming this attempt to be successful then when the time comes that the fields of biology and physiology have been completely explored, the corresponding aspect of psychology would be reduced to the status of a mere corrollary of a precise physiological representation. But, supposing that when the field of experimental investigation has been completely explored there should still remain a factor, which should prove not amenable to scientific measurement, but which should yet prove vital to the understanding of behaviour, then psychology might claim that in respect of this factor it must be allowed to evolve a new method of attack. There was a time when the suggestion that ' emotion, character and will ' should ever be expressed in terms of a mathematical equation would have been greeted with derision. But this time has passed. The 'faculties' have disappeared from psychological writings, the concept of an abstract 'will' has been replaced by that of 'willed action' (in which apparent mere interchange of terms, there is a profound significance), and 'emotion' is discussed mainly in connexion with glandular reaction. The psychologist is showing an increasing disposition to incorporate in his work to the fullest extent the results of physiological research as it affects the reaction of behaviour, and to present an unalarmed front to the possibility of ultimate solution along these lines alone. He may feel that in the meantime, pending the complete exploration of the physiological field which alone can resolve the problem, that his particular function is to work out in the field of behaviour those items which can be isolated for immediate investigation, and to ensure that the overlapping of different manifestations receives due recognition. We may perhaps be entitled to say that the object of psychological investigation is to express behaviour in terms of the least number of independent variables. It must also elucidate the relationships between the factors which it is found necessary to assume at the different stages of the investigation. If, in the last resort these minimum factors should prove to be purely physiological then the mechanistic school may claim to have justified itself, but if there comes a point at which the physiological explanation breaks down it should then become apparent why the scientific method must also fail in its attempt to crystallize the whole.

We are familiar in the history of the physical sciences with the method which is known as the making of relevant abstractions. We realize that in every science the first development ensued as the result of an accumulation of data. Kepler, for example, collected data about the motions of planets and as the result of his analysis formulated certain empirical laws. It was left to Newton to make the abstraction which regarded the earth as a point and the sun as a centre of attraction, and so to draw his conclusions. When the question of the mechanism of the tides was under investigation, the earth was considered simply as a rotating sphere covered by liquid, with the sun and moon as centres of attraction. On the analysis of this problem, the heaping up of the water under attraction was deduced. But for other purposes the earth is regarded not as a sphere, but as a spheroid. The point which would appear to emerge is that the nature of the abstraction is dictated by the needs of the problem in hand, and that the nature of the problem is derived from the consideration of the data which are available. Psychology is considered to be at the best a young science. It may be said to be still at the stage of accumulating data, and the 'relevant abstractions' have yet to be made. It would be possible to hazard conjectures as to the lines along which they will have to emerge. Some writers in the psychological field may claim that they have already made their selection and are working up to the formulation of their laws. In the final issue it will remain to be shown that the results which accrue from one abstraction do not invalidate those of the others.

Surveying the problem from the scientific angle we may feel intimidated by the extent of the field, and the enormity of the task. There is perhaps one small aspect of it which suggests itself as requiring urgent consideration. We refer to the criticism as to looseness of terminology to which allusion has already been made. It must be recognized that the criticism is just. Not only, it is argued, does the connotation of terms used, vary in different psychological text books, but the issue is further complicated by the fact that many of the terms are taken from common speech and have already a vague significance. It is, for example, disconcerting to the layman to learn that while he may know broadly what he may mean when he speaks of the ' disposition ' of a companion, the psychologist wishes to restrict the meaning in the exposition of his subject. That the psychologist is justified in such a restriction, there can be no doubt. It may perhaps be found advisable, in the interests of accuracy to devise a new terminology to meet the needs of psychological expression. Such a procedure might, in appearance at least, tend to make psychology more detached from those problems of life and behaviour, which are supposed to be its peculiar province. But we must be prepared to make the subject technically invulnerable, and if it is found that a terminology divorced from that of common speech is required in order to give precision to the ideas involved, the necessity must be faced. Other sciences have had to overcome the same difficulty.

It is easy to select examples of topics, proper to

psychological inquiry, in which the progress of elucidation has been severely handicapped by this
looseness of usage in respect of the terms employed.
To the writer of this monograph it appears that the
subject of 'temperament' affords a most cogent
instance. From the time of Hippocrates 'temperament' has figured in philosophical and psychological writings as one of the constituents which
determine behaviour. The language in which it
has been treated has been vague and obscure, and
this, combined with the equally indeterminate
associations which are carried over from the speech
of every day life, have contrived to surround the
subject with an atmosphere of unreality which is
in sharp contrast to the significance of the rôle
assigned to it. It is withal a subject which has
its own appeal. All that is attempted in the following pages is to give a short historical outline
of the treatment which 'temperament' has
received at the hands of psychological theory. The
resulting conflict in expression and significance
will be only too apparent. It is hoped that this
attempt may lead to an ultimate precise definition
of the factor involved. If this should prove possible
it would then be necessary to investigate experimentally the claim of such a clarified concept to
inclusion in the irreducible constituents which
determine behaviour. If on the other hand we
find on analysis that 'temperament' has no
meaning, other than that covered already by better
defined terms we must be content, as far as
psychological inquiry is concerned, to eliminate
it altogether.

CHAPTER II

CONFLICTING DEFINITIONS OF
TEMPERAMENT

IT has been suggested in the previous chapter, that the study of the theories of temperament, which have been put forward from time to time, offers a most cogent example of confusion resulting from the use of ill-defined terms attached to nebulous conceptions. An attempt is here made to investigate some of the available theories with a view to elucidating if possible any common factors which may emerge.

In common speech temperament is held to possess a determining influence upon behaviour. To ascribe a man's conduct to his temperament is to make a certain gesture of dismissal which refers to the adjudged finality of the temperamental factor. The phrase 'the victim of his temperament,' expresses a general belief that whatever the temperament may actually be, it is liable at any time to upset the more orderly components of a man's personality.

Again we hear frequently the expression ' incompatibility of temperament.' This suggests that the influence of temperament makes itself felt in the relations of people, one to another, and that where this mysterious incompatibility occurs, it constitutes a real and vital obstacle to profitable relationship. Again, there is the idea of finality and the conception of temperament as a rigid, implacable force, working destructively. It is significant that in common speech temperament is most frequently invoked in excuse for failure in adaptation to external demands. One even hears the adjective 'temperamental' applied loosely without context. To say that so and so is 'temperamental' is to make a statement partly derogatory, and partly pitying in character—which implies that so and so is unreliable—moody—and erratic in behaviour. It is less easy to find in popular speech a phrase which would seem to give a more positive and hopeful turn to the temperamental factor. Certainly the phrase 'he has the artist's temperament' may be spoken in approbation, but more generally it is in apologetic defence in excuse of some slight deviation from conventional conduct. While one hears frequently the remark, 'he is temperamentally incapable,' of following a particular line of action, it is seldom thought necessary to bring forward the more positive aspects of the subject's temperamental outfit.

There is, however, also to be met with—though less frequently—an attempt at a somewhat less vague classification of temperament. Thus it is not uncommon to hear an individual referred to as being of a sanguine, a nervous, or of a morbid temperament. One hears also the words phlegmatic, melancholic, choleric on the lips of people who would lay no claim to the study of the psychological history which produced these terms. It may be supposed that the terms here indicated supply a means of expression for the observed differences in individual behaviour. It may be not unprofitable to consider the nature of the differences symbolized vaguely by the above mentioned ' types of temperament.' It is difficult at this stage to clear one's mind entirely from any more circumscribed connotation which one may perhaps wish at a later stage to impose on a particular term. If we select for example the 'morbid temperament' for examination we have here a term which has no exact classical counterpart. It would appear to denote something rather more than the allied term melancholic. The individual marked down as morbid would probably be further described as reading into his experiences a subjective reference not easily understood by more so called ' normal people.' The word ' unhealthy ' would probably be employed in this connexion and the subject would be described as preoccupied with the darker side of life. At the opposite end of the scale would be put the man of ' sanguine' temperament who would be described as taking life easily and maintaining an equable reaction to its emergencies. The same description would perhaps apply also to the phlegmatic, but he would be marked off from the sanguine as altogether less vital and possibly as less lovable. Without further analysis of these terms as commonly employed, it may perhaps be claimed that they represent an attempt to interpret behaviour and to find, if possible, some more or less constant factor in the individual which makes itself felt in reactions which may be themselves different.   The problem may be briefly stated thus. Changing situations will provoke different reactions from the same individuals, but can any factor or factors be isolated of which the influence is seen in the widely differing reactions.   If so then it may be possible to investigate it, and it may be referred to conveniently as the ' temperament ' unless it is thought advisable in the interests of peace to introduce a new term, which simply by virtue of its newness, will prove to be less controversial.

With this problem in mind the inquirer turns to the text books of Psychology in the hope of finding there a clear cut definition of temperament which may help in his investigation.   He will at once perceive that, grouped round the word temperament in psychological writings, are the terms ' instinct,' ' disposition ' and ' character.'   The controversy as to the number, grouping and hierarchy of the primitive instincts is still raging.   The very existence of instincts is threatened, but whatever may be the ultimate decision on this point the connotation of the term in modern psychological writings is circumscribed.   Thus we may quote McDougall's definition of an instinct as an— ' innate disposition which determines the organism to perceive (to pay attention to) any object of a certain class, and to experience in its presence a certain emotional excitement and an impulse to action which find expression in a specific mode of behaviour in relation to that object.'[1]   On this basis he distinguishes a man's ' disposition ' as the

---

[1] Outline of Psychology, page 110.

sum total of his instinctive tendencies, and the
' temper ' of a man as ' the expression of the way
in which the conative impulses work within him.'

He then goes on to say ' The temperament of a
man may be provisionally defined as the sum of
the effects on the mental life of the metabolic or
chemical changes that are constantly going on in
all the tissues of his body.'[1]   We are not at the
moment concerned with the validity of these
definitions but with the contrast in degree of
explicitness which they present. An instinct may
be what McDougall claims it to be and on that
basis the ' disposition,' may, if the psychologist
wishes it, become the sum total of instinctive
tendencies. But we cannot feel that the tentative
definitions of ' temper ' and ' temperament ' carry us
much further in the understanding of their functions.

An attempt to connect temperament and character in one definition is often made. A. F. Shand,
for instance, speaks of the temperament as our
innate character, and goes on to say, ' Thus the
temperament is that part of the innate constitution
of the mind which is different in different men so
far as this refers to their feelings, and perhaps
also to their wills.'[2]   Tests of temperament and
character are bracketed together in the recently
published report of the Consultative Committee of
the Board of Education on Psychological Tests of
Educable Capacity.   In the same section ' temperament and will ' and ' temperament and emotion '

---

[1] Outline of Psychology, page 354.
[2] The Foundations of Character, page 128.

are spoken of together and no distinction is made between them. Woodworth speaks vaguely of the 'sort of trait that we think of under the head of temperament' and Watson denies any psychological significance to the term. Maher in his chapter in ' Rational Appetency' writes, ' The total collection of a man's acquired moral habits grafted on to his natural temperament makes up his character. The original element in so far as it is determined by his bodily constitution was called the temperament by the ancients. The ancient physiological explanation has long been abandoned, but the classification has been generally retained.'[1] On the surface this may appear to form a connecting link between the definitions of McDougall and Shand quoted above.

Experience suggests that if a clear cut definition of temperament cannot be obtained it is at least possible to emphasize one aspect in its consideration. Whatever the temperament may be it is a differentiating agent and whether its connexion is primarily with emotion or not, its effect must be looked for in the reactions of behaviour.

When Maher speaks of a man's ' natural temperament ' and Shand of our ' innate character ' they imply that it must be considered as given at birth. They would appear to give sanction to that idea of finality which we saw to be bound up with the popular conception. The whole question of whether or not temperament is subject to modification is an interesting one which engaged the thoughts of men many centuries ago. But its consideration involves

---

[1] Psychology, page 391.

the whole question of the supposed connexion between temperament and bodily constitution. Maher wrote that the ancient physiological explanation has long been abandoned, but the idea of some physiological explanation has by no means been abandoned. In the definition given by Dr. McDougall it was seen that the chemical changes in the body are supposed to exert an influence on mental life. A very definite theory as to the exact nature of the influence of bodily changes on mental processes is now being vigorously put forward in the modern doctrine of endocrines. 'The internal secretions' says Mr. Louis Berman in his book 'The Glands Regulating Personality' 'constitute and determine much of the inherited powers of the individual and their development.'[1]

Again 'The internal secretion formula of an individual may in the future constitute his measurement which will place him accurately in the social system.'[2]

The exponents of this theory hold out hopes of such control of mental development by the regulation of the ductless glands as will finally remove from the temperament its incalculable nature.

It may then be profitable at this stage to postpone for the time being the question of cut and dried definitions and to investigate that aspect of the problem which deals with its physiological basis. This will take us back to the times when men first began the attempt to distinguish between types of 'individuals.'

---

[1] The Glands Regulating Personality, page 23.
[2] Ibid, page 23.

CHAPTER III

THE CLASSICAL DOCTRINE OF THE TEMPERAMENTS

BRETT in his ' History of Psychology ' says, ' The first object of interest to man is not the soul but the person.' The ancients were quick to realize the differences between men and between races. ' The strong will, the fiery spirit, the crafty mind, all appear as types of men.'[1] ' The first step in the evolution of theories, was the discovery that man is subject to laws, not of his own making. Man discovers that he is part of a universe, that his very motives and dispositions are subject to laws and can be treated as universals, that training, dietary and habituation make him master of himself. To the student of human nature apparently so spontaneous and original in its manifestations it must have been a great revelation to realize that behind this complex being there was a world of elements and that the very nature of man, his temperament, passions and thoughts could be controlled by those who knew the secrets of climate and food. Climate and disposition, food and morals, the humours of the blood and errors of thought, these are the terms in which the relation

---

[1] History of Psychology, pages 8, 9.

between macrocosm and microcosm are continually stated and re-stated.'[1]

To Parmenides mind was the product of the material composition of the body. Empedocles held that the four elements—Air—Water—Fire—Earth—were the essential factors, and that the union of these elements in varying proportions determined the individual existence.

In this simple theory we see the basis of the idea that individual characteristics depend upon a quantitative physical mixture. Hippocrates, writing in the fifth century B.C. elaborated it from the standpoint of the physician with a view to elucidating the conditions which govern health.

Starting with the four elements of Empedocles—Earth—Fire—Water and Air—he considered the four corresponding qualities—Cold—Hot—Moist and Dry. By combining these qualities two and two he arrived at the four corresponding humours, viz.,—

Blood, the combination of the hot and the moist.

Phlegm or Pituita, the combination of the cold and the moist.

Yellow Bile, the combination of the hot and the dry.

Black Bile, the combination of the cold and the dry.

He held that these humours flowed from the brain and that their bad admixture was the cause of all diseases. He used the term ' The Mixture ' to denote the proper mingling of the humours in a state of health.

The two influences to which the humours were particularly susceptible were, according to Hippo-

---

[1] History of Psychology, pages 19-20.

crates, diet and climate. He observed that corresponding to the combinations of the four qualities which determined the humours themselves were four similar combinations which determined the seasons of the year.

Thus. Hot and Moist combine in the Spring.
Cold and Moist combine in the Winter.
Hot and Dry combine in the Summer.
Cold and Dry combine in the Autumn.

He pointed out that the greatest opposition is between the combination Hot and Dry and the combination Cold and Moist, and that therefore the two humours of which the action is most sharply opposed are the bile and the phlegm, so that an excess of either produces grave disease.

So, each season has its particular humour. Thus in the Spring the blood, in the Summer the bile, in the Autumn the black bile, and in the Winter the phlegm are to the fore and each season has accordingly its particular diseases.

It is through the medium of climate that Hippocrates traces the effect of his combinations on the health and character of individuals and races. Just as the seasons were determined by the possible associations of the four qualities, so are the climates of different regions. In his treatise on ' Air, Waters and Places ' he says :

' For where the changes of the seasons are most frequent and most sharply contrasted there you will find the greatest diversity in physique, in character and in constitution.'[1] Again speaking

---

[1] Air, Waters and Places, § xxiv.

of the inhabitants of countries of extreme climate
he says : ' The heads of the inhabitants are moist
and full of phlegm and their digestive organs
are frequently deranged from the phlegm that
runs down from the head. Most of them have a
rather flabby physique and are poor eaters and
drinkers.'[1]

With regard to the lack of spirit and of courage
among the inhabitants of Asia, the chief reason why
the inhabitants of Asia are less warlike and more gentle
in character than Europeans lies in the uniformity
of the seasons which show no violent changes
either towards heat or towards cold, but are equable.

Galen, five hundred years later elaborated the
ideas of Hippocrates and introduced many more
possible combinations in different degrees of the
four fundamental qualities. ' In this way,' says
Brett, ' the psychology of character was combined
with the physiology of temperament, and anger,
fear and hope became effects of the material constitution of the body.'[2]

Galen had to take into account the development
of philosophy since the days of Hippocrates and more
particularly the doctrine of the soul and the pneuma
but he maintains that the doctrine of the ' mixture '
is equally valid here.

' The essence of the soul is also a mixture either
if you like of certain elementary qualities—moisture
—dryness—cold—and heat—or if you prefer of
elementary bodies—the moist—the dry—the cold—

---

[1] Air, Waters and Places §iii.
[2] History of Psychology. Vol. I., page 289.

the hot.' This distinction may not appear to us to be as vital as it was to Galen, but we have to remember that he was concerned with the manufacture of certain ' psychic spirits,' which should bridge the gap between what was physical and the less tangible outcome of a man's spirit. He allocated to the liver the production of 'desire' in virtue of its close connexion with nutrition; intellect fell naturally to the brain while ' temper ' which he identified with vitality was produced by the ' spirits of the heart.' The measure in which these ' faculties ' as they might not unjustly be called in Galen's view were related to one another constituted the nature of the individual.

Two points which Galen makes are of special interest to modern inquiry. He insists that it is only on this basis of temperament that individual differences can be explained and also that only through the temperament can the acknowledged influence of wine and drugs on mental life be understood.

' Those who think that the soul is not helped or hindered by the temperament of the body have nothing to say of the differences between children and can give no reason for the diversity of manner which makes some bold and others cowardly, or some intelligent and others stupid.'[2] Again, 'Men are not born all the enemies nor all the friends of right ; the good and the bad are such as they are

---

[1] Chales Darenberg. Oeuvres traduites de Galenus. Ch. III., page 55.

[2] Oeuvres traduites de Galenus. (Darenberg). Ch. XI., page 91.

because of the temperament of the body.'[1] Galen gives in much detail the variations in physical appearance which he believed to be determined by the mixture of the humours, and he elaborated the ideas of Hippocrates as to the influence of climate.

If we pass over a thousand years, we find that the classical doctrine of the temperaments had remained fundamentally unchanged. Certain points, as for example the exact seat of the humours and more important still, the claim of the black bile to an independent existence were in dispute but the main contention remained unaltered. So in 1621 Burton in his 'Anatomy of Melancholy,' wrote:—

'Of the parts of the body there be many divisions; the most approved is that of Laurentius out of Hippocrates, which is into parts contained or containing.

'Contained are either humours or spirits.

'A humour is a liquid or fluent part of the body and is either innate or born with us or adventitious and acquired.

'Blood is a hot, sweet 'temperate' red humour prepared in the meseraick veins and made of the most temperate parts of the chylus in the liver whose office is to nourish the whole body.

'Pituita or phlegm is a cold and moist humour begotten of the colder part of the chylus (or white juice coming out of the meat digested in the stomach) in the liver; his office is to nourish and moisten the

---

[1] Oeuvres traduites de Galenus (Darenberg) Ch. XI., page 84.

members of the body, which are as the tongue moved.

'Choler is hot and dry, bitter, begotten of the hotter parts of the chylus and gathered to the gall; it helps the natural heat of senses. Melancholy, cold and dry, thick, black and sour, begotten of the more fœculent part of nourishment and purged from the spleen is a bridle to the other two hot humours, blood and choler, preserving them in the blood and nourishing the bones. These four humours have some analogy with the four elements and to the four ages in men.'[1]

From this train of thought, shadowed by Empedocles, developed by Hippocrates and refined by Galen there emerged that classification of men into sanguine, choleric, melancholic and phlegmatic which still retains its hold. 'The ancient physiological explanation' wrote Maher, 'has long been abandoned but the classification has been generally retained.' Common speech supplies us with examples of its use, and we may conclude that this denotes the measure of a need fulfilled. For its inclusion in modern psychological writings we must I think accept the verdict of Dr. E. Webb when he writes—

'Among abstract propositions put forward by theologians, teachers and psychologists many writers have issued classifications of the temperaments. They are remarkable for the frequency with which they reach the ancient and time honoured

---

[1] Anatomie of Melancholy. Pt. I. Section I. Member II. Subsection II.

four-fold classification of temperaments—sanguine melancholic — choleric — phlegmatic. But the apparent unanimity is merely superficial. While adopting the terms to signify four types they vary as widely as possible in the meanings they attach to them and in the explanations offered.'[1]

The fact that it has proved possible to harness this ancient classification in support of so many different investigations of psychological types must in itself indicate the vagueness of the mental characteristics which were attached to a comparatively well defined physical basis. If we wish to understand the nature of the types which belong properly to the ancient classification before it had become overlaid with modern theory we may turn to Richerand's ' Elements of Physiology.' Richerand writing in the eighteenth century had ceased to stress the humoral foundations and contented himself with this explanation—' The predominance of any particular system of organs modifies the whole economy, impresses striking differences on the organisation and has no less influence on the moral and intellectual, than on the physical faculties. This predominance establishes the temperament, it is its cause and constitutes its essence.'[2]

He then proceeds to a detailed description of the five temperaments, (the extra one has crept in with the admission of the claim of the black bile to a separate existence). His observations are given in his own words and comment for the moment is reserved.

---

[1] Character and Intelligence, page 2.
[2] Physiology §231.

I. SANGUINE.

' If the heart and vessels which carry the blood are of predominant activity the pulse will be sharp—frequent—the complexion ruddy, the countenance animated, the forms softened though distinct—the hair fair, the nervous susceptibility will be lively ; men of this temperament will pass rapidly from one idea to another : conception will be quick, memory prompt, imagination lively ; they will be addicted to the pleasures of the table and of love and will enjoy a health seldom interrupted by disease.

The ancients applied the name of sanguine to this disposition of the body, and considered it as produced by the combination of warmth and moisture and had very correctly perceived that it existed in the young of both sexes and was modified by the spring.

The physical traits of this temperament are found in the statues of Apollo of Belvedere ; its moral physiognomy is drawn in the life of Mark Antony.

Inconstancy and levity are in fact the chief attributes of men of this temperament ; good, generous, quick, impassioned, delicate in love and fickle.'[1]

II. BILIO

' If sensibility which is vivid and easily excited can dwell long upon one subject—the pulse strong,

---

[1]Physiology §231

hard and frequent—the skin brown—the hair black, moderate fullness of flesh—the passions will be violent, the movements of the soul often abrupt and impetuous, the character firm and inflexible. Bold in the conception of a project—constant and indefatigable in its execution—it is among men of this temperament that we find those who in different ages have governed the destinies of the world. Such were Alexander, Julius Caesar, Cardinal Richlieu.

As love in the sanguine, so ambition is in the bilious, the governing passion.

An excessive development of the liver, a remarkable superabundance of the biliary juices most commonly accompanying this constitution of body, the ancients gave it the name of bilious.' [1]

III. MELANCHOLIC.

When to the bilious temperament is added diseased obstruction of one of the organs of the abdomen or derangement of the functions of the Nervous System, so that the vital functions are feebly or irregularly performed, the general uneasiness affects the mind, the imagination becomes gloomy, the disposition suspicious ; the exceedingly multiplied varieties of this temperament called by the ancients the melancholic, justify the opinion that the melancholic is less a primitive and natural constitution than a diseased affection hereditary or acquired.

Distrust and fearfulness, joined to all the dis-

---

[1] Physiology, § 233.

orders of imagination compose the moral character of this temperament.

The history of men celebrated in the sciences, letters and arts, has shown us the melancholic under a different light. No one perhaps has ever shown the melancholic temperament to a higher degree of energy than the philosopher of Geneva. Till the time when impelled by the desire of fame, Rousseau sprang forward in the career of letters, we see him endowed with the sanguine temperament acting with all the qualities belonging to it—gentle —loving—feeling—though inconstant, but gradually undeceived by the hard lessons of experience, afflicted in the depths of his heart by his own wretchedness and the wrongs of his fellow creatures, his bodily vigour wastes and decays. With it his moral nature changes and he may be referred to as the most striking proof of the reciprocal influence of the moral on the physical and the physical on the moral part of our being.' [1]

IV. PHLEGMATIC.

' If the proportion of the fluids to the solids is too great the superabundance of the humours which is constantly in favour of the lymphatic system gives to the body considerable bulk. The flesh is soft, the countenance pale, the form rounded and without expression, all the vital actions more or less languid, the memory treacherous, the attention not continuous. Men of this temperament to which the ancients gave the name of pituitous, and we should call lymphatic, have in general an insurmountable

---

[1] Physiology, § 234.

c

inclination to sloth. Little fitted for business they have never exercised great empire over their fellow creatures.

Among the moderns Michel Montaigne—all whose passions are so moderate, who reasoned on everything, even on feeling, was truly pituitous. But in him the predominance of the lymphatic system was not carried so far, but that he joined to it a good deal of nervous susceptibility.' [1]

V. THE NERVOUS.

' The property by which we are more or less sensible to impressions in our organs—weak in the pituitous—moderate in those of sanguine temperaments—rather quick in the bilious—constitutes by its excess the nervous temperament—seldom natural or primitive but commonly acquired and depending on a sedentary and too inactive life. This temperament shows itself in emaciation—in the smallness of the muscles—in the vivacity of the sensations, in the suddenness and mutability of the determinations and judgements. This temperament has never shown itself, but among societies brought to that stage of civilization in which man is the farthest possible from nature. The two most remarkable men of the eighteenth century, Voltaire and the great Frederick, may be given as instances of the nervous temperament, and the history of their brilliant and agitated life shows sufficiently how much the circumstances in which they lived contributed to develop their native dispositions.' [2]

---

[1] Physiology, § 235.
[2] Ibid, § 236

For the purpose of comparison Richerand's classification may be tabulated as follows :—

Temperament.	Physical Characteristics.	Mental and Moral Characteristics.
1. Sanguine.	Fair Complexion and hair ; healthy	Easily affected, inconstant, good memory, fond of pleasure and variety, marked by wit rather than genius.
2. Bilious	Skin dark, hair black.	Impetuous, violent passions, indefatigable, ambitious.
3. Melancholic.	Nervous system deranged, vital functions feeble, not a primitive temperament.	Suspicious, gloomy and disordered imagination but capable of producing genius.
4. Phlegmatic.	Pale, flabby, languid.	No concentration, bad memory, lazy, may be joined with nervous susceptibility
5. Nervous.	Small frame and muscles.	Vivacious, inconstant, great nervous susceptibility.

There can be no doubt that Richerand gives us a recognizable description of types of men. Let us ignore for the moment the differences in physical appearance which are claimed to correspond with the temperamental types, and try only to concentrate on the differences in behaviour which the types would indicate. It will be remembered that we set out with the hope of being able to isolate certain factors in behaviour, which by their constant manifestation in different reactions might claim to be regarded as unit characters. Now Richerand gives us a plentiful though vague choice of such characters, and they combine to present a more or less complete picture of the man. Without attempting to impose upon him too much of the trend of modern theory we may perhaps be justified in claiming that from his vague and general characteristics one or two stand out in comparative clearness. One of these would seem to be a variation in speed of reaction, and another the variability in maintenance of reaction at its original level. There is also to be discovered a reference to a third factor which we may for the moment call ' emotionality.'

The same distinction may be recognized in the classification drawn up as late as 1892 by Dr. A. Stewart. He was concerned with an attempt to revive interest in the old classical doctrine, which, he claimed should be of profound significance alike to the doctor, the phrenologist and the educator. It will be noticed that he differs from Richerand in the value he attaches to the phlegmatic or lymphatic and to the nervous temperament. He also omits altogether the melancholic temperament. ' As there are not two kinds of bile, black bile being only concentrated yellow bile, the melancholic (atrabilious black bile), temperament has no sufficient claim to be classed as one of the four temperaments, and has given place to the nervous.'[1]

---

[1] Our Temperaments, page 21.

His classification is as follows :—

Temperament.	Physical Characteristics.	Mental and Moral Characteristics.
Sanguine.	Complexion florid, eyes blue, face square, build thickset.	Impulsive, cheerful, excitable, ardent not persistent, muscular rather than intellectual.
Bilious.	Complexion dark, eyes dark, face square, build thickset.	Passionate, jealous, persistent, unscrupulous, well informed, prefers business pursuits.
Lymphatic.	Complexion pale, eyes lustreless, build thickset.	Slow, heavy, not excitable, persistent, not ardent, plodding, fond of personal comforts.
Nervous.	Complexion clear, eyes grey, face tapering, neck long, build slight.	Impulsive, excitable, imaginative, enduring in work, enjoys intellectual and muscular pursuits.

The chief point of interest is perhaps, as has been suggested, the high degree of value which he attaches to the nervous temperament. An attempt to bring the doctrine into line with modern science may be traced in his suggestion that if the law of the survival of the fittest could be applied in this sphere it would act in favour of the nervous temperament, which he says, is the intellectual and refining temperament as opposed to the three others. He quotes from Sir J. Crichton Browne's Book of Health—' From the nervous to the lymphatic temperament through the sanguine and bilious and other intermediate temperaments compounded of these, there is a gradual diminution in the rate of nerve action and in the fineness of quality of nerve substance.'[1]

Stewart dwells also on the balanced temperament —the ' Mixture ' of Hippocrates and endorses the claim of Hippocrates as to the modifying influence of food, climate and race.

At this stage of the inquiry we must appear to have wandered far from the comparatively simple relation first propounded between the humours of the blood and varieties of behaviour.   The tables drawn up after the classifications of Richerand and Stewart give the supposed corresponding visible characters of external appearance.   The belief that much of a man's personality may be roughly deduced from his physical exterior is widely held, and the attempt to establish this belief on a scientific basis has occupied scientists in many ages.   A most interesting account of the latest work in this direction is given in Dr. E. Miller's little book ' Types of Body and Mind.'   In his chapter on the morphological aspect he makes special references to Kretschmer's classification into two main types— the Pyknic and the Asthenic, with its subdivision of the athletic.   But in our present investigation we must be content to leave out of account this fascinating field of work, and concentrate upon the physiological rather than upon the morphological aspect.   Our immediate object is to look for

---

[1] Quoted ' Our Temperaments', page 136.

variation in behaviour ; such variation may be connected definitely with differences in structure, but the aim of this chapter has been rather to present the different theories of variation in bodily functioning, which in turn lead to differentiation in behaviour.

The progress of the sciences of physiology and medicine led inevitably to the abandonment of the doctrine of the humours of the blood. Richerand, as we saw, had ceased to stress the humoral foundation in his account of temperament. We can find traces of attempts to connect the temperaments with the action of the nerves and of the muscles, but the most modern counterpart of the doctrine of humours is undoubtedly to be found in the theory of the endocrine glands. To the consideration of this theory, and its connexion with the problem of temperament we must now turn.

CHAPTER IV

TEMPERAMENT AND THE ENDOCRINE GLANDS

IT is necessary at this point to resist the temptation to set down at once the attractive classification of 'endocrine personalities' outlined by Dr. Louis Berman in his book, 'The Glands regulating Personality.' In juxtaposition to the tables of Stewart and Richerand, given above, Dr. Berman's classification might be used to emphasize either the continuity of the type idea, or the contrast in physiological basis on which it is supposed to rest. But the value of such emphasis would at this stage tend merely to falsify the conception of the value of modern research on the endocrine glands. It would reduce to another mere speculative hypothesis work which though far from complete can justly claim to be considered on the basis of an exact science.

It is now generally admitted that the endocrine glands, or glands of internal secretion exercise a far-reaching influence upon the general economy of the body. As to the general nature of this influence we cannot perhaps do better than quote the words of Dr. E. Miller. ' The rôle of the endocrines,' he writes, ' is a twofold one in which the two-sidedness is in essence undivided biologically ; it is only methodologically two fold. On the one hand we shall find that their functions are intimately related to metabolism and growth ; on the other hand, they are concerned with the organism in its external relationships, that is, with the emotional reactions that are associated with the life of instinctive adjustment to external situations (by instinctive adjustment we mean, in its widest sense, the satisfaction of interests by contact with environment). Growth of body and adjustment are reciprocally related to one another so intimately that the two fold function of the endocrines is in reality but one final response of the organism—the act of living.[1]

If this verdict can be shown to be true, then the importance of the endocrine theory in the consideration of temperament will also be established. But in order that we may not, in a moment of over enthusiasm, be led to impose on the theory, corollaries which it may prove incapable of supporting, it is necessary to begin by an attempt to disentangle from the increasing volume of literature on the subject of endocrinology those factors which can lay claim to scientific demonstration, and which at the same time would appear to have an intimate connexion with the problem which confronts us. We are reminded by Dr. Miller that the books which have been written about the endocrine glands, display in some cases an enthusiasm which has not an exact correspondence with scientifically established facts.

---

[1] Types of Mind and Body, page 42.

' But so great have been the interest and enthusiasm for research upon the glands of internal secretion, and so great the wish for a solution of all physiological problems on the basis of their activity that hypotheses have outrun facts. The experiments themselves, because of the complexity of their factors, have led to very contradictory results. Fortunately with the subsidence of the flood of literature, a not entirely barren country has made its appearance, upon which a few tender facts are seen to have been established.' [1]

We must therefore, concentrate for the moment upon the plain unelaborated statement of what is actually known about the glands and their function. The terms used are ' endocrine glands ' or glands of internal secretion. The active agents secreted by the glands are referred to as hormones unless the alternative term of autacoid, used by Professor J. B. Watson, is preferred. These organic substances, when secreted, pass directly into the circulatory fluid and produce demonstrable effects upon other organs. The group of endocrine glands includes—

    i. The Thyroid (with the Parathyroids).
    ii. The Suprarenals.
    iii. The Pituitary.
    iv. The Pineal.
    v. The Thymus.
    vi. The interstitial cells of the sex glands.
    vii. The Pancreas.

Of these the first three have been studied in more detail than the others, and it is customary to attach

---

[1] Types of Mind and Body, page 41.

to them a superior rôle. The line of investigation into the work of the ductless glands involves :

(a) the isolation of the hormone.
(b) the study of the effect of removal of the gland.
(c) the effects of increased and diminished activity.
(d) the effects of injection of the secretion.

From investigations of this nature an idea of the exact function of the gland in question may be obtained. The results obtained by experiments on these lines in connexion with the separate glands are given below.

A. THE THYROID SYSTEM.

The thyroid system (including the four parathyroids), is situated on either side of the wind pipe, and its secretion, thyroxin is known to contain a percentage of iodine. The effect of the removal of the thyroid gland is to arrest the growth of the skeleton and of the cells of the cerebral cortex. Similarly a diminished action of the thyroid is marked by a definite slowing down of the processes of metabolism and a consequent arrest of growth with diminution of sex function. The conditions of cretinism and myxœdema are associated with the atrophy of the thyroid apparatus. Conversely a hyper-thyroid condition is indicated by a lowered blood pressure, and increased nervous excitability ; and the administration of thyroxin in cases of hypothyroidism has been found to produce a general increase in the rate of metabolism and to serve as a corrective to the arrest in development which accompanies this condition.

B. The Suprarenal System.

The adrenal glands are attached to the kidneys and must be distinguished in respect of two parts —the cortex and the medulla. Little is known about the cortex, and its secretion has not been isolated, but it is believed to have a close connexion with sex functions. The hormone of the medulla is known as adrenin and its direct function appears to be the conversion of liver glycoyen into sugar.

The removal of both adrenal glands in animals produces death. A study of the effect of degeneration of the glands (the condition occurring in Addison's disease), shows that it is accompanied by general debility and loss of muscular tone. The effects of the administration of adrenin have been found to consist in a rise of blood pressure and a slower action of the heart. It is believed that the work of the suprarenal glands is connected with the regulation of sugar and of fat, that is, with carbohydrate metabolism. Evidence is also forthcoming to show that in certain mental disorders, as for example anxiety states there is excessive blood sugar and a correspondingly high blood pressure. One of the most valuable investigations of the working of the suprarenal glands has been that of Dr. W. Cannon who has demonstrated their action in assisting to dispel fatigue. The results of a series of experiments on the administration of adrenin are given in his book ' Bodily Changes in Pain, Hunger, Fear and Rage.' It is not possible to give the details of his experiments, but he claims to have distinguished as the result a four-fold function of adrenin which becomes operative in emotional excitement and in the resistance of fatigue. This function may be summarised as follows—

(1) it can set free an increased supply of sugar from which the organism can draw additional muscular energy when faced with an emergency.

(2) it can stimulate a fatigued muscle to better response and so again increase the muscular power at the disposal of the organism.

(3) it can cause the withdrawal of blood from the abdominal viscera into the organs upon which the greatest demands are made in an emergency situation.

(4) by increasing the speed of the coagulation of the blood, it retards the loss of blood.

C. THE PITUITARY APPARATUS.

The pituitary is a small organ at the base of the brain and here also a distinction must be drawn between the anterior and posterior lobes. The secretions of these lobes are known respectively as tethelin and pituitrin. The effect of the administration of pituitrin is seen in increased blood pressure and a lowering of the rate of the action of the heart. A state of under-activity of the posterior lobe results in obesity and arrest of sexual development, and it is supposed that the activity of the secretion of this lobe has a special connexion with the action of the reproductive organs and with the activities of other glands. Hyper-activity of the anterior lobe appears to result in a general enlargement of the bones, particularly those of the hands and feet and it is deduced that the influence of its hormone upon metabolism has a direct connexion with the growth of the skeleton.

D. PINEAL AND THYMUS GLANDS.

Little is known about the exact functions of these glands, and the nature of their secretion has not been isolated. Their influence appears to be felt mainly during childhood, and it is surmised that their function is the prevention of a too rapid maturing of the reproductive organs. Their work should normally cease after puberty and it has been observed that a persistent thymus is frequently associated with a diseased pituitary gland.

E. SEX GLANDS.

In so far as the internal secretion is concerned, we need consider only the interstitial cells. They secrete a hormone which influences bodily development and more particularly the secondary sex characteristics. For the purposes of our consideration their chief importance lies in their very close relationship to the work of the thyroid and suprarenals on the one hand, and to the pituitary on the other. This brings up the whole question of the inter-relations of the systems of ductless glands.

We have so far limited ourselves to the barest physiological statement of what may definitely be claimed to be known about the isolated action of the various endocrine glands. It must appear that this crude outline gives no hint of the possibility of the determining rôle which was ascribed to the glands at the beginning of the chapter. Some explanation is now required of the manner in which the functions of these glands are related amongst themselves and also to the unified functioning of the body. It will be remembered that the rôle of the endocrine glands was outlined as two-fold.

(a) in relation to problems of metabolism and growth.

(b) in relation to adjustment to external environment.

It was also emphasized that this two-fold function is in reality only two aspects of a single process, and the key to their unification is provided only when we consider together the work of the endocrine glands and of the nervous system.

We are accustomed to consider the Central Nervous System as the supreme agent of integration. In recent years we have seen an increasing emphasis laid upon the importance of the Vegetative system, and in virtue of its recognized precedence in time, we have correspondingly exalted its functional importance. According to Professor J. B. Watson, ' There has been a tendency in recent years to exploit the sympathetic system at the expense of the cerebro spinal. This has been done largely in the interest of giving a neurophysiological basis to certain psychoanalytic principles.'[1]

A more correct estimate of the respective rôles of these systems is that which recognizes that the two nervous systems together with the endocrine gland system form a co-operative whole which regulates the growth of the organism, and its responses to the external environment. While the central

---

[1]Psychology from the standpoint of a Behaviourist, page 171.

nervous system is concerned pre-eminently with response to the environment, that response is connected directly with body metabolism through the agency of the vegetative system and the endocrine glands. The case for this co-operative action has been well put by Dr. Miller. He writes :—

' The endocrine system with its vegetative nervous connexions, is the link between metabolic processes and the highest neural and psychical processes. The latter possess immediacy of response by a complex of reflex activities and mental associations ; the endocrine system has the inertia necessary for keeping in time with established metabolic activities. The endocrines therefore, translate the tempo of the nervous system into the tempo of metabolism. In linking metabolism and growth to the life of external adjustment the endocrines speed up the one and give inertia to the other.'[1]

In order to obtain a more complete understanding of the link between the vegetative nervous system and the endocrine glands, it is necessary to consider the division of the former into the sympathetic and parasympathetic systems, with mutually antagonistic action. It has been demonstrated by carefully devised experiment that individuals tend to vary in the degree of irritability of these two systems in the presence of certain stimuli. An excessive irritability in respect of the parasympathetic system has received the name vagotonia while conversely an over activity of the sympathetic system in similar conditions is known as sympatheticotonia.

---

[1]Types of Mind and Body, page 45.

It now remains to inquire, in view of these ascertained facts what is the particular relation of the different endocrine glands whose function we have outlined to the work of the vegetative nervous system. One of the most striking facts which will arise in this connexion is the close relationship which exists between the thyroid and suprarenal systems. We have seen that the effect of administration of thyroid extract was to raise the level of metabolic processes, and the conservation of the increased heat so produced is more particularly the work of the suprarenals and is effected through the constriction of the arterioles of the skin. Both the thyroid and suprarenal secretions appear to have a direct effect upon the sympathetic nerve endings. The connexion between the two systems is summed up by Dr. Miller in these words :—

' If thyroid sensitizes sympathetic nerve endings it produces a greater rapport with the external world. If it sensitizes sympathetic nerve endings it would in accordance with the work of Tournade and Chadral produce an increased output of adrenin by increasing the sensitivity of the splanchnic. Hence increased thyroid action leads to increased suprarenal activity and hence to increased glycoyen output from the liver. In this sense it is a heat regulator in so far as increase of circulating sugar increases the fuel of the muscles. This heat must not be dissipated for the energy needs of the body are greater with increased demand of the external world for active response. But the increased adrenin also constricts the arterioles of the skin, and hence inhibits the loss of heat : thus energy is

D

conserved for action.'[1] ' In this way the demands
of the external world are met through the first
metabolic relay station, the thyroid gland. . . .
Hence a well-tuned thyro-suprarenal system is one
of quick response and rapid metabolic interchange."
. . . Further the thyroid hormone exercises an
excitatory influence on the vegetative centres for
the expression of emotion in mesencephalon and
diencephalon, above all on those centres which
concern fear, anxiety and anger. It may thus be
regarded as sympatheticotonic. It may be possible
that in states of mental uncertainty and of conflict, there is a state of disharmony produced
between the thyroid and the suprarenal bodies,
with the result that there is a state of physiological
uncertainty producing alternating vascular changes
seen in the hot and cold flushes of anxiety states
and during the height of the climacteric.'[2]

The conclusion reached by Dr. Miller is that the
condition described above as sympatheticatonic is
accompanied by increased activity of the thyroid
and suprarenal systems and in consequence by a
more rapid response to external demands.

In contradistinction to the close alliance between
the thyroid and suprarenal systems, no such intimate
connexion can be established between either of
these glands and the pituitary.

The facts which have been put forward concerning
the functioning of the chief endocrine glands are
such as may claim to be established on a true

---

[1] Types of Mind and Body, page 60.
[2] Ibid, page 62.

scientific basis. No attempt has so far been made to infer from them general types of behaviour, or to connect them directly with what is understood by mental processes. Once or twice the use of the word 'emotion' has crept in in the quotations given, but the exposition of the theme of emotion will require a separate chapter. It is now open to us to consider the views advanced by different writers as to possible correlations between endocrine activity and types of behaviour. The most enthusiastic and entertaining of such views are put forward by Dr. Louis Berman in his book, 'The Glands regulating Personality' but it may be well to begin with the statement made by Dr. Leonard Williams in the medical section of the British Journal of Psychology for July 1922. He writes:—

'In the scale of evolution, the brain and higher centres of the spinal cord are mere mushroom growths compared to our visceral ganglia and practically coeval with them are the glands of internal secretion.

'While the time is not yet ripe for dogmatic statement, there is a large mass of evidence which goes to show that the ductless glands constitute the mainspring of this surprising mechanism. Nor does the importance of the endocrines stop here, for according to the exact proportion in which their essences are admixed in your blood you are tall or short, dark or fair, phlegmatic or choleric, saint or sinner, sexual, homosexual or sexless, male or female.

'Even the least experienced of us can claim to

some extent to judge a person's character by his outward seeming, his voice, his gesture, his shape and colour, and his eyes. If therefore, you grant to the endocrines the responsibility for the one, the other follows as a matter of course. If man's conduct is determined by his endocrines, so also is his character, for character is only conduct so often repeated as to become habitual.'

Below is given the table of endocrine glands, their secretion and function, drawn by Dr. Berman, and it is followed by a second table based upon the main features—' Physical—Mental and Moral,' which he claims to belong to ' types ' which in turn owe their existence to the predominating activity of one particular set of glands.

DR. BERMAN'S CLASSIFICATION.[1]

Gland.	Secretion.	Function.
Thyroid.	Thyroxin.	Gland of energy production. Controller of growth of specialised organs and tissues—of brain and sex.
Pituitary		Gland of energy, consumption and utilization—continued effort.
2 lobes.		
Anterior.	Tethelin.	Growth of skeleton and supporting tissues.
Posterior.	Pituitrin.	Nerve cells and involuntary muscle cells.

[1] Glands regulating Personality, page 94.

Gland.	Secretion.	Function.
Adrenals.		Gland of combat.
Cortex.	Unknown.	Brain growth; over-development of sex glands.
Medulla.	Adrenalin.	Energy for emergency situations.
Pineal.	Unknown.	Brain and sex development—adolescence and puberty, and maturity.
Thymus.	Unknown.	Glands of childhood.
Interstitial Glands of	Testes in male. Ovaries in female.	Glands of secondary sex traits.
Parathyroid.	Unknown.	Controller of lime metabolism ; excitability of muscle and nerve.
Pancreas.	Insulin.	Controller of sugar metabolism.

On the basis of this classification Dr. Berman draws up a list of endocrine personalities, the main characteristics of which are given in the following table.

Type.	Physical Appearance.	Mental and Moral Characteristics.
Thyroid.	Fair—nose straight healthy, good teeth, thick hair, bright eyes.	Not subject to fatigue, rapid perception and volition, tendency to explosive crises of expression.
Adrenal.	Skin pigmented, hair thick and dry.	Vigorous, persistent, successful, efficient, has to meet shocks of life.

Type.	Physical Appearance.	Mental and Moral Characteristics.
Pituitary.		
(a) Anterior pituitary.	Good growth and harmonious function.	Excellent brain power, masculine type, great self-control.
(b) Posterior pituitary.	Slight and delicate, creamy complexion.	Susceptible to tender emotions, feminine type.

If we subject these tables to a rigorous analysis in the light of the preceding account of the work of the endocrine glands, and if we leave out of account (in the absence of conclusive scientific evidence in its support) the description of the accompanying physical features, we are struck by the fact that while in respect of certain broad principles Dr. Berman's classification is in harmony with the foregoing account, he yet appears to read into these principles indications of detailed behaviour which we cannot as yet accept as single factors dependent upon the relative functioning of the glands. When, for example, he speaks of the thyroid as the gland of energy production, and of the suprarenals as the glands of combat, we can, in virtue of what is known about the influence of these glands on metabolism, accept this description. We can, in this connexion, even leave uncriticized the use of the term 'energy', since it apparently implies no more than the crude bodily energy liberated in the form of heat. Grouping together his descriptions of the ' mental and moral characteristics' which are supposed to accompany the thyroid and adrenal types, we see here a picture of an individual whose adjustment to the external world, other things being equal, would be rapid and vigorous and this again would accord with the view already quoted that a ' well tuned thyro-suprarenal system is one of quick response and rapid metabolic interchange.' We must, however, decline at this stage, to admit ' rapidity of volition,' as a valid inference and reserve for further inquiry the ' tendency to explosive crises of expression,' ' Volition ' is too complicated to be considered as a single independent factor, and its possible connexion with temperament will be dealt with later in reference to Ach's well known work on this subject. As to the whole question of emotion, perhaps the most difficult of psychological topics, but one which a consideration of temperament must of necessity include, that, as has been suggested must be reserved for a special investigation.

In view of the present incomplete state of knowledge of the working of the pituitary glands we must be content to preserve an open mind as to the ultimate possibility of their being correlated definitely with such factors as ' self control,' or of ' susceptibility to the tender emotion.' The suggestion made by Berman, that the pituitary is to be looked upon as the gland of consumption of energy, as opposed to the function of the thyroid in producing energy is interesting.

' While the thyroid increases energy evolution and so makes available a greater supply of crude energy, by speeding up the cellular processes, the pituitary assists in energy transformation, in energy expenditure and conversion—especially of the brain and sexual system.' [1]

---

[1] Glands regulating Personality, page 68.

This suggestion would appear to accord with the view already indicated that there is a certain antithesis between the rôles of the pituitary and of the thyroid glands, but until the phrase 'energy expenditure and conversion' can be translated into more precise metabolic language, we must beware of attaching too much importance to it. The notion of a trinity in respect of production, conservation and conversion of energy, paralleled by the functionings of the thyroid, suprarenal, and pituitary glands, is a fascinating one for the psychologist, but in the pursuit of scientific method he must beware of its misleading facility.

We do not wish to imply that in working out his alluring sketch of endocrine personalities Berman has limited himself to the expression of crude statements, based merely upon fanciful hypotheses. He gives in fact a detailed description of each gland and of its supposed effects upon personal appearance and mental life, and he emphasises the details of their common application in all individuals. He supports this choice of extreme types by reference to figures of history who would appear to fit in well with the description he gives. But the method of illustrating psychological types by reference to men prominent in history, art, or science, is itself open to criticism. In such cases the deductions made are from the known record of the individual's life more particularly as exemplified in his greatest works, that is to say, in works for which the conditions were themselves of a highly specialized nature. The proof of a temperamental type must surely be sought in the presence of a constant

factor which makes itself felt in reactions, which
themselves vary with the particular conditions
obtaining.

Dr. Berman has an easy manner of disposing of
radical difficulties. He supplies for example the
link between temperament and instinct in the
form of the adrenals.

'The James-Lange theory of emotion regards it as
a consciousness of the very changes in the organism
which adrenalin causes. Since adrenalin is the
starter of the whole process and since McDougall
has defined an emotion as the feeling aspect of an
instinct, just as an instinct may be defined as the
motor aspect of an emotion, the adrenals as emotion
genetic and instinct genetic play a part in the
most profound processes of the subconscious and
unconscious.'[1]

The tale of the ductless glands as told by Dr.
Berman does not stop at the specific functions of
their different secretions. As part of the vegetative
system he identifies them with the oldest basis of
mind itself, and claims that the currents which arise
from them set up the 'stream of feeling which constitutes the undertow of consciousness.' These
currents vary in size, position, and warmth, and these
aspects are embraced by the term 'tonus.' This
tonus can be measured quantitatively and he gives
an approach to a mathematical formula for its
computation.

'The pressure within a viscus is dependent
upon the ratio between the amount of contraction

[1] Glands regulating Personality, page 110.

of the involuntary muscles in its walls, the external pressure, and the quantity of its distending contents. The resultant quotient—the internal pressure divided by the external pressure measures the intravisceral pressure. The primitive wish feelings are the expressions of the various intravisceral pressures or tonus.'

This leads up to his definition of character as the ' grand intravisceral barometer.'[1]

The question must now arise, 'How much further has this consideration of the work of the endocrine glands taken us in our inquiry ? ' We may perhaps say that it has established beyond question the relationship between the functioning of the glands, the general metabolism of the body and the adjustments of the organism to environment. It has shown that individuals differing in respect of activity of specific glands, or in irritability of the sympathetic and parasympathetic nervous systems will show evidences of this variation in their reactions. While we may feel hopeful that a more complete knowledge of the work of the endocrine glands may in time elucidate to a much greater extent the nature of these corresponding differences in reaction, we must admit that at the present time it is impossible to lay down with certainty any basal types. We may however, with some degree of confidence, claim that the evidence in hand points to an ultimate demarcation on the lines of speed of reaction, possibly also to a differentiation in regard to persistence of reaction.

---

[1] Glands regulating Personality, page 106.

CHAPTER V

TEMPERAMENT AND EMOTIONALITY

IN the foregoing accounts of the classical doctrine of the temperaments and of the modern theory of endocrine glands, an effort was made to pass over, without emphasis as far as possible, the connexions which were postulated between physiological conditions, and what is generally known as the emotional life of the individual. In spite of this precaution such references inevitably crept in. We saw for example that Richerand, speaking of the bilious temperament, attributed to it ' violent passions,' that the sanguine was labelled ' feeling though inconstant,' while Stewart spoke of the sanguine as ' ardent not persistent,' and of the bilious as ' passionate and jealous.' Berman referred to the post—pituitary type as ' peculiarly susceptible to the tender emotions, and to the thyroid type as ' liable to sudden crises of emotional expression.'

If these references were for the moment relegated to the background it was not because their importance was underestimated but because we have in this topic of emotion perhaps the most intransigeant subject of psychological investigation. It is unlikely that any conception of temperament which eliminates the emotional aspect will ever prove an acceptable basis of definition. Feeling is indissolubly connected in popular imagination with the idea of temperamental differences, and before we can proceed to the consideration of temperament as an aspect of character, in which connexion it is invariably used in modern psychology, an effort must be made to reach at least a partial understanding of the rôle of emotion in behaviour.

The questions which confront us may perhaps for the purposes of our investigation be reduced to two. First, can any meaning be attached to the phrase that people vary in respect of what is often termed, 'general emotionality,' and secondly, is there any evidence to show that variabilities in emotional reactions can be correlated amongst themselves to an extent which would point to a general factor in this respect. But as a preliminary to this investigation it would be necessary to consider some of the existing hypotheses as to the nature and function of emotion or perhaps more correctly of the emotions.

Controversies about the emotions have so far centred round the following points—

(1) Are the emotions to be considered as antecedent or consequent to behaviour reactions ?

(2) To what extent is an emotion the result of a curtailed reaction ?

(3) Are we to believe that the bodily changes which we know to accompany the expression of an emotion are in reality the constituents of the emotion ?

The case for the last of these three points is of

course embodied in the famous ' James-Lange ' theory of emotion which is summed up by McDougall in these words. ' The essence of this theory is the assertion that the ' emotions ' are essentially of the same nature as ' sensations,' that an ' emotion ' as felt or an emotional quality, is a mass or complex of confused sensory experiences arising from the sensory impressions made by the processes going on in the various organs of the body, and that each distinguishable quality of emotion owes whatever is specific or peculiar in its quality to the specific conjunction of sensory activities, the visceral organs playing a predominant part in this sensory stimulation.'[1]   James himself writes—

' If we fancy some strong emotion and then try to abstract from our consciousness of it all the feelings of its bodily symptoms we find we have nothing left behind.'[2]

The theory would then appear to reduce itself in its simplest form to a statement of this nature.   A stimulus occurs—a reaction follows—and the bodily changes attendant on these reactions (or at least some of them) are experienced by the subject as an emotion.   If this were all then we must judge that the importance of emotion is greatly overstated. We are accustomed to think of an emotion as itself a driving force to action.   This is probably due to the fact that we associate it with a profound disturbance, the more profound because, although we recognize certain localized bodily symptoms, as for example the trembling of the limbs, and the

---

[1] Outline of Psychology, page 326.
[2] Psychology.   Shorter Course, page 379.

more rapid beating of the heart, we yet believe that its effects are in reality more far reaching than this. Woodworth, who defines an emotion as the stirred-upness, present in a state of mind, and as an essentially conscious quality, makes the difficulty of localization the essential criterion in the diagnosis of an emotion. It is this he says which differentiates for example a genuine emotion from hunger and thirst, which are generally recognized as akin to, though not identical with, emotion proper. Woodworth goes on to say, that while hunger, which he defines as an organic state, results from an internal bodily process, the existing cause of an emotion is usually something external, but that organic changes, in the presence of an emotion, can be definitely observed and that the disturbance caused by these changes does in all probability constitute the emotion. Further, that the organic changes, one aspect of which is experienced as an emotion, are in reality in the nature of the preparations for some overt action, and that emotion is in fact always accompanied by some characteristic external movement. ' The conscious state of being afraid is composed of the sensations of trembling and of muscular and glandular responses.'[1]

It is in these words that Woodworth sums up the James-Lange theory and he points out that the only really satisfactory test of the theory would consist in the cutting off of sensations from the trunk, in which case the emotional quality of the experience should, if the theory be correct, disappear.

---

[1] Psychology, page 129

If we are content for the moment to abstract from the James-Lange theory the admitted truth that bodily changes are at least an important constituent of emotion, we realize at once the close connexion which exists between such changes and the working of the suprarenal glands. Attention was called to the experiments of Cannon in this respect, and also to the apparently close relationships of the thyroid-suprarenal systems. We might therefore conclude that, viewing the problem from the opposite angle, it would be true to state that one effect of the working of this particular glandular system is undoubtedly to be found in emotional experience, and that therefore the more actively this system functions the stronger we might expect the emotional experience to be. But to take over at once such a simplified hypothesis would lay us open to the charge of attributing causality of emotion to the working of the glandular systems, whereas, as was pointed out by Woodworth, the assumption is that external causes are the initial producers of emotion. It would also mean that we are ignoring the charges brought against the James-Lange theory as a complete explanation.

In reviewing alternative theories of emotion we may perhaps limit ourselves to the versions given respectively by the behaviourist school of psychologists and by those who emphatically deny this position. Mr. J. B. Watson who defines an emotion as an 'hereditary pattern reaction' involving profound changes of the bodily mechanism as a whole, but particularly of the visceral and glandular systems, yet thinks it necessary to add in a footnote that he is not striving to reduce the emotions to pure physiology, but merely to connect emotional activity with physiological processes since this connexion is now established as a practical fact. He goes on to say (and this may prove to have a direct and important bearing upon our particular problem) that such hereditary patterns appear to get broken up as life proceeds, and only emerge in their original form in very abnormal circumstances. A description of adult behaviour, from the emotional angle would probably refer to what Watson calls the general activity level of the individual's behaviour. His conclusion on this head may, in view of its importance, be stated in full. ' Observation would seem to suggest the following formulation. Organized activity (hereditary and acquired) may go on and usually does go on at a given level. We may call the most usual the normal level of equilibrium. It varies with different individuals and one can determine it even with respect to a single individual only after observing him for a considerable time. We may note further that an individual at one time may exhibit more energy, punch or pep, than the normal, for example, during and immediately after a cold shower. We may call this the excited level. Again at times he works at a level lower than normal, for example, when in trouble, after money losses or illness ; we may call this the depressed level.'[1]

' Without neurologizing too much, we may venture the assumption that in adults the environ-

---

[1] Psychology from the Standpoint of the Behaviourist, page 218.

mental factors have brought about the partial inhibition of the more external features of the primitive pattern types of emotion. The implicit, mainly glandular and smooth muscular side of the pattern, remains. The emotionally exciting object releases important internal secretions, which without initiating new (part) reactions reinforce or inhibit those actually in progress. This hypothesis would account for changes in level. Only in rare cases do we see mere changes in level. Usually, when such changes occur, certain auxiliary or additional part reactions appear, such as we see in whistling while at work, keeping time with the feet, drumming on the table, biting the finger nails.'[1]

This conception of a general level of activity varying in different individuals, and in the same individual at different times is an attractive one from the point of view of the temperamental problem. It is, on the surface similar to an idea put forward by some writers of a stream of ' psychic energy ' varying in volume and rate of flow. But it would at this point be a mistake to read into the theory of a general level of activity, as expounded by Watson, any such general hypothesis. His views may perhaps be reduced to this very simple statement. His investigations of the reactions of infants —made under conditions approximating closely to those of the laboratory—led him to believe that reactions corresponding to what we call fear, rage, and love (in the Freudian sense of the term), may be evoked during the first few months of the child's

[1] Psychology from the Standpoint of the Behaviourist, page 218.

E

life, and that therefore, presumably, such reactions are unlearned. On the basis of these three original 'emotional patterns' the other recognized emotions are built up by processes of combination and transference, but the details of these operations do not concern our present problem. The important point would appear to be that in general the emotional disturbance is inseparable from some form of activity, (which, in the case of the three original 'emotion reaction patterns,' outlined above, would be termed instinctive activity), but that environmental conditions and social pressure lead, at an early age, to the repression of the complete overt action appropriate to the stimulus. While vestiges of such action remain the effect of the bodily changes (mainly visceral), resulting from the emotional stimulus, is seen in the ordinary activities of the individual rather than in any specific action. Such diffusion of affect is not, Watson points out, always uniform, but in virtue of the particular interests or circumstances of the individual may incline unduly in one direction. Hence we get the phenomenon of substituted outlets, of phantasies, and, in acute cases, of neuroses. In the light of this explanation meaning could be attached to such phrases as 'emotional pressure,' 'emotional drainage', tension and relaxation. But what meaning, if any, could be found for the expression 'high' or 'low' general emotionality? Here it seems, so far as our investigation has at present carried us, is the crux of the whole question. If, using Watson's terminology we speak of a high level of activity it would signify that the implicit reactions to the emotional stimul have been more or less evenly distributed (without encountering repression), but that susceptibility to such stimuli was high and the total change produced before its affect was distributed was also high. On the other hand, we should have to take into account the comparative duration in time of the increased activity level. It is probable that a combination of highly increased activity level and shortness of its duration, would indicate a meaning for 'high emotionality.' But would the converse statement be equally true ? A sudden lowering of activity might equally be the result of an emotional stimulus. Similarly we might connect the term, 'high general emotionality,' with a readiness to display the accepted external signs of specific emotions and it is undoubtedly true that to many people the phrase 'highly emotional' conveys this meaning. We feel, then, that at this stage we cannot dogmatize upon the question of 'general emotionality,' but must be content to say that judged from the angle of attack, outlined by Watson, the possibility of the existence of such a factor is not at least ruled out.

But we must now take into account the views of those writers, who differ fundamentally from the behaviourist standpoint. We may perhaps take McDougall as the typical representative of this school. While he is careful to deprecate the tendency, observable in some psychological writings to personify the emotions, he yet attributes to them a more dynamic rôle than has hitherto been suggested. He ascribes to emotional experience a three-fold character—the quality of the emotion, the exper-

ience of bodily characters—and a conative factor.
Now we have seen that Watson himself emphasized
the inseparable connexion between emotion and
action, but McDougall would appear to mean something more than this. Conative behaviour in the
sense of persistent striving is, he says, ' indicative
of an energy which works teleologically and which
is therefore radically different from the energies of
physical science '—Conative experience is the felt
impulse to action and such impulse is present in all
emotional experience—If the conative factor
could be subtracted from an emotional experience
that experience would be radically altered—The
only way to account for this impulsive power of the
emotions is to recognize that all the bodily changes
of any species of animal which we call ' the expression of the emotions '—are adaptations of the body
to modes of instinctive activity proper to the
species.[1]   We may contrast this with the three
original emotion reaction patterns of Watson, but
fortunately, for the problem which we have in hand,
the vexed question of the number, grouping, and
hierarchy of the primitive instincts and their
emotions is not of paramount importance and need
not detain us here.   McDougall affirms that the
functions of the primary emotions is to indicate
to the subject the nature of his excitement, and
the kind of action to which he is impelled.   In
virtue of this function he regards them as the
' cognitive basis of self knowledge and self control.'
He criticizes the James-Lange theory of emotion.

---

[1] Outline of Psychology, page 317 et seq.

on the ground that conative and sensory experience cannot be identified, and that, if the sensational qualities were cut out of an emotional experience through anæsthesia of the whole body, the remaining experience would not be purely cognitive since the specific emotional quality might be centrally excited. It is conceivable, that, as was suggested by Woodworth, the conflicting truth in the statements of Jones and McDougall in this respect may eventually be resolved by laboratory experiments.

It will be seen from the above quotations that the radical difference between McDougall and Watson seems to lie in the hypotheses of a purposive rôle of the emotions. This is made still more clear by McDougall's summing up of his own criticism of the James-Lange theory. Putting these criticisms together, I would say, that while James's theory is fundamentally correct, his statement of it errs in implying a more intimate dependence of our mental processes upon bodily changes than is actually the case. Further he ignores the conative factor, the part of impulse in emotion considered either as a phase of experience or as a phase of behaviour. He ignores the fact that an impulsive striving towards a goal is the essence of every emotional reaction. When we say ' I feel angry ' and explain our striking at an offender by saying ' I struck because I was angry ' we do not mean that the emotional quality of our experience was the active agent that caused the striking ; rather we mean quite properly that the being angry does, as a matter of empirical fact and experience involve an impulsive tendency to strike ; and our explanation is true and valid. We implicitly use the emotional quality that we recognize, as the indicator of the instinctive tendency that has been aroused in us. Hence the ordinary statement ' I struck because I was angry ' is essentially truer, gives a truer explanation of any action, than James's inverted statement ' I am angry because I struck.' [1]

The last allusion to the controversy as to the priority in time of reaction and emotion, would appear to have little bearing upon our present problem. It is however, linked up with the very much larger problem of interdependence of bodily and mental reactions. McDougall as we have seen, claims that he is not attributing causality to the emotions but at the same time, claims the complete interdependence of mental and bodily states. Watson on the other hand simplifies his problem by ignoring the existence of such a difficulty. We may prefer the one or the other line of approach, but we must at least realize that the recognition of this cleavage in point of view is fundamental to the understanding of the rôle of emotion in the writings of different schools of thought. Those who, like the psycho-analytic school of thought, speak of the ' libido ' and of ' primitive urges,' are clearly basing their doctrine upon the hypothesis of a stream of energy, which they call psychic, the behaviour of which is analogous to that of the more easily observed physical energy. Their reply to the attack of the physicist is that even though such energy may not be measurable in clearly defined

---

[1] Outline of Psychology, page 328.

units, the postulation of its existence is nevertheless justified in view of the practical success of the resulting technique. This may well be so, but the fact remains that in our attempt to find temperamental characteristics we shall do better to concentrate upon observable differences in reaction rather than on mere differentiating hypotheses. What would appear to happen is that an attempt to differentiate on the basis of the libido leads inevitably to a very broad and general classification. This we see to be the case in the 'Psychological Types' of Jung which we must later take into account.

There is however, another aspect of the working of emotion which is emphasized by some psychologists notably by Dr. Drever, viz., that an emotion is only experienced as such when the action appropiate to the stimulus is checked. Such an arrest of the impulse to action is then said to produce tension which is experienced in the form of an emotion. In accordance with this view, would be Dr. Burt's definition of emotion as 'the conscious aspect of a curtailed instinct.' The majority of people would probably confirm the truth of this statement, at least to the extent of assenting that the more the action is curtailed the more strongly the emotion is experienced. The emotion of anger would perhaps be the readiest illustration in this respect. We have also seen the same idea underlying Watson's theory of the distribution of affect corresponding to a blocked outlet.

Reference was made at the beginning of the chapter to the question of the existence of a factor of general emotionality. We saw that the so

called ' level of activity,' postulated by Watson,
might have an important bearing on this point.
An interesting contribution to the subject is made
by Dr. Cyril Burt, as the result of his investigation
of delinquent children. He came to the following
conclusion—' In actual fact, as statistical analysis
has proved, an excessive liability to one particular
instinct tends (at all events as a general rule, though
not of necessity in any single individual) to be
accompanied by a liability, more or less excessive
to most of the remainder. The correlation is clearer
among children than among adults and among
delinquent children that among virtuous. The boy
who steals is nearly always secretive, usually
disposed to petty sexual faults ; often a truant ;
not infrequently quarrelsome and spiteful and
yet sometimes incongruously enough an arrant
coward, an easy dupe, spasmodically generous,
warmly affectionate and prone to heartbroken tears
of remorse. Thus as with intellectual capacities
so with emotional ; a single central factor pervades
them all. The central factor underlying intellectual
processes has been described as " general intelligence." The central factor underlying instincts
and emotions may be termed "general emotionality"
and persons whose general emotionality is developed
to an exceptional degree may be designated technically
unstable.'[1]

On this hypothesis there would be in every
individual some inherited mechanism which would
constitute a central emotional core, from which the

---

[1] The young Delinquent, pages 506-507.

quality of emotional experience would either become differentiated into specific emotional experience varying with the nature of the stimulus or would at least be available to reinforce such specific emotions.

In this rapid review of differing embodiments of the theory of emotion, we have omitted many points which may appear relevant. There is, for example, the question of the measurement of emotion. It must be felt by many that if we can reply to the scientists, that we have a machine for measuring emotion, whether it be the galvanometer or another, they will automatically treat our efforts with greater respect. This is probably true, but the most enthusiastic supporter of measurement in psychology, would readily admit that in respect of emotion the machinery is not as yet very efficient and that in consequence the time for it to be brought forward in argument has not yet come. Another point we might have dealt with is the question of affective tone.

If the idea of positive or negative affective tone, given in Whateley Smith's ' Measurement of Emotion ' is adopted then the final result of the affective tone is either to attract or repel attention, and so facilitate or impede the rise of an idea to consciousness. A positive affective tone is held to produce a relaxation of tension and so to become in the first place synonymous with pleasure. Its action would therefore tend to be a reinforcing one.

But throughout the chapter we have been concerned primarily with the fundamental differences in point of view, which make emotion the subject of such contradictory theories. We can see that these differences group themselves in the first place into biological or non-biological and again into dynamic or static. If, on the other hand we prefer to seize upon the points of agreement we find them to consist in the acknowledgment of the close connexion which exists between the experience of emotion, and the organic changes resulting from the stimulus, and in the admission that between the intensity of experienced emotion and efficiency of overt action the correspondence would appear to be inverse.

CHAPTER VI

TEMPERAMENT AND TEMPER IN MODERN PSYCHOLOGY.

MODERN psychology of the pre-endocrine gland period, was wont to consider temperament as an aspect of character. We saw the reference outlined in Maher's definition, but the most detailed and valuable treatment in this connexion is undoubtedly that given by Mr. A. F. Shand in his work 'The Foundations of Character.'

His definition of temperament as our 'innate character' has been quoted, and it is significant that he emphatically rejects the classical doctrine of the tenperaments as a basis on which the scientific study of character can be built up. He gives an analysis of the classical doctrine quoting Richerand, Stewart and Fouillée in its support, and he then lays down three important defects which render it scientifically useless. These defects are :—

(1) that such qualities as superficiality, slowness, etc., can be inferred in all mental processes of a person who inherits any one of the temperaments.

(2) that they are based on conceptions of quantities which are indefinable in amount.

(3) that they are artificial and exaggerated and do not represent the real temperament of men, *i.e.*, most men have mixed temperaments.

Now Shand regards the specific emotions as essentially dynamic in function, and as the most powerful central factor of instinctive activity. ' The emotions,' he says ' are forces and we have to study them as such. Our analysis must not be preoccupied by their constituent feelings and sensations—and it is here that they are little capable of scientific treatment, because these constituents are so elusive and variable,—but must be directed to show what are their main tendencies, what biological value they have at first, and what value for the higher ends of character afterwards.'[1] And again in criticism of the James-Lange theory he writes—

' It is a remarkable fact that two writers, so original and independent could only discern this physiological problem, that James looked upon it as the one way he knew of to lift the study of the subject out of barren classification and description, while there was the familiar and far more important problem before them, with which practical men are in some measure conversant of the part which these emotions play in human life. If these primary emotions belong to our mental constitution, they would presumably not belong to it unless they had some biological value . . . The biological conception of the emotions now carries us but a little way. Man does not merely, like the animals, live that he

---

[1] Foundations of Character, page 1.

may preserve his life and that of his species.   As we rise above primitive forms of emotion a number of ends come into prominence that are concerned with the welfare and happiness of life rather than with its preservation.   As James and Lange did not envisage this problem, so they did not consider the bearing of their physiological theory on the conception of the emotions as forces unconsciously pursuing ends . . . A later and more fruitful point of view is opened up by the study of the connexion between the emotions and the principal instincts . . . By the recognition of the active side of the primary emotions, we are once more able to regard them as among the fundamental forces at the base of character, and the study of them on their dynamical side as affording, through the comparatively simple problems they present, the most hopeful line of advance to the more involved problems of the science.'[1]

Starting with the primary emotions enumerated by McDougall, Shand gives an interesting account of their interaction and organization into the major sentiments of the character.   But such organization is, he maintains, definitely influenced by two innate factors, viz., temper and temperament. We observed above the distinction drawn by McDougall in respect of temper and temperament. ' The temper of a man seems to be the expression of the way in which the conative impulses work within him,'[2] and ' The temperament of a man may be provisionally defined as the sum of the effects

---

[1] Foundations of Character, pages 1-8.
[2] Outline of Psychology, page 353.

upon his mental life of the metabolic or chemical changes that are constantly going on in all the tissues of his body.'[1] Shand claims no distinction in quality between the two, but suggests that while 'temper' is applied to the workings of a particular emotion, the term 'temperament' is used in a more comprehensive sense in reference to the emotional nature in general. 'Thus we speak of even, excitable, and violent temperaments—but of an irascible temper. From this point of view a man's temperament is the sum of the innate tempers of the different emotions.'[2]

From this statement, it is clear that Shand regards men as differing in what is popularly known as their susceptibility to particular emotions. In slightly more psychological language we might say that the same stimulus will provoke differing degrees of emotional experience in different men. It may be replied that in later life at least this will be influenced largely by the associations aroused by the stimulus. Psycho-analysis would add to this that the degree of emotional disturbance produced is also dependent upon the extent to which freedom of expression of emotional reaction has prevailed.

Shand admits that in respect of at least two of the primary emotions—fear and anger—differences in susceptibility may be observed in young children, but he points out, as would appear to be indisputable, that it is not, in our present stage of experimental knowledge, possible to say definitely whether this increased or diminished susceptibility

---

[1] Outline of Psychology, page 354.
[2] Foundations of Character, page 129.

is in reality innate or the result of early environmental influences. In later life such differences are even more apparent, and with changing tempers of specific emotions he would be inclined to group changing temperament. He does not, in fact, recognize in it a unifying principle. 'While the tempers of men are thus subject to great changes in the course of life, the temperaments are supposed to be constant. Emerson has even represented them as an inner destiny against which it is vain to contend. This is an exaggeration since nothing which is concrete is exempt from change.'[1]

As Shand lays down as one of his fundamental laws of character that the sentiments tend with increasing success to control the emotions, it would appear from his conclusions that the formation of character should normally tend to obliterate the traces of temperamental differences.

Of the three criticisms raised by Shand against the old classical doctrine of the temperaments, and quoted above, the first one, the charge of superficiality, is clearly fundamental. He treats in some detail of the qualities of instability and intensity of feeling which were supposed to characterize respectively the sanguine and the bilious temperaments. In reference to the sanguine temperament he writes : ' We have only to assume that this quality of superficiality is universal and attaches to all systems of the character for the statement to be generally true of all those who possess this temperament and in whom it is not counteracted. It is a character-

---

[1] Foundations of Character, page 131.

istic part of the doctrine of the temperament to make such an assumption that because a certain quality is manifested on one side of the character, therefore it will be manifested on all sides.'[1]

Emphasizing this point again in connexion with the alleged irascibility of the bilious temperament he says—' That the irascible temper is innate there can be little doubt, but is it the sign of a temperament? That is to say if a man shows a hasty and superficial temper, can we infer that all his other feelings will be correspondingly hasty and superficial? Admitting this, can we infer that where this discrepancy exists it is due to some counteracting cause? But what is the nature of this counteracting cause, unless it be that the irascible man in respect of some other emotion or some sentiment may manifest an opposite innate disposition.'[2] He finds the same ground for objection in the analysis of the nervous and lymphatic temperaments in the assumption that the quickness of the nervous or the slowness of the phlegmatic pervades the intellectual processes as well as the emotions and sentiments. His contention that slowness of mental processes and bodily movements are due rather to deficient energy or specific disease appears to connect easily with the endocrine doctrine.

His final conclusion is this—' The doctrine of the temperaments does not then give us grounds for extending our inferences beyond these limits which our observations of the individual in question justify.'[3]

---

[1] Foundations of Character, page 133.
[2] Ibid, page 135.
[3] Ibid, page 131.

It is clear that in Shand's view the issue appears to be the extent to which high degree of susceptibility to one emotion carries with it a correspondingly high susceptibility to another. It will be remembered that as a result of his investigation of delinquent children Dr. Burt found in fact that excessive liability to one form of instinctive reaction was found to be accompanied by increased liability to certain other forms. It was upon this observed fact that he based his hypothesis of a central emotional factor.

The foregoing account of the emotions and their rôle may appear to have been unduly abstract. In the discussion of particular emotions we have a field of universal appeal making essentially for concrete and attractive treatment. But in taking account of conflicting theories of emotion we have felt compelled to neglect this admittedly more attractive side. In our search for a constant, temperamental determinant, we are concerned chiefly with the problem of the existence of a ' general emotionality ' factor or at least of the overlapping of emotional constituents. We have seen that psychologists are not agreed about its possibilities, but it would appear to be pre-eminently a subject of experimental investigation, and it may be that in the course of a few years a more unqualified pronouncement may be made on the subject. If, with Mr. Shand, we are not prepared to grant the existence of a central emotional core then the temperament will be limited to the mode of expression of each individual emotion, that is to its ' temper,' and scientific investigation of the emotional

F

aspect of temperament will be based on the attempt to elucidate what Shand calls ' the degree of sensibility to an emotion.' We may now proceed to ask in what way such susceptibility will show itself. Two considerations present themselves. In the first place, there is the initial speed of reaction to an emotional stimulus, and in the second, the length of duration of emotional disturbance. A third term is suggested in the conception of ' intensity ' of emotion. ' Intense ' as opposed to ' superficial ' is perhaps the adjective most commonly applied to the description of an emotional reaction, but if we try to analyse the meaning of intensity in this connexion it reduces itself to the question of duration in time and to the extent to which ordinary activity is interfered with by the emotional disturbance. Now such interference would be manifested partly by expressive movements of the body and partly by the speeding up or paralysis of ordinary activity. That is to say we are brought back to Watson's description of the general activity level.

A somewhat analogous conception is worked out by Fouillée in his ' Tempérament et Caractère,' a work which is quoted by Shand in his criticism of previous theories of temperament. Fouillée is himself an adherent of the classical doctrine in a somewhat revised form; that is to say, he contrives to give to his exposition of it a turn which seems to bring it much more closely into line with modern psychological thought. He writes :—

' *Entre l'action des choses ou des hommes sur nous et la réaction par laquelle nous y répondons, il y a toujours un intermédiare, notre tempérament qui produit ce qu'on a si bien nommé notre indice de refraction mentale . . . Le tempérament, c'est la caracteristique dynamique d'un individu. . . . Nous avons des tempéraments d'épargne et des tempéraments de dépense, les uns en prédominance d'intégration les autres en prédominance de désintégration.'*[1]

M. Fouillée himself divides the temperaments rather according to the slow or quick reaction, and inclines to the division into ' *les vifs,*' ' *les lents,*' *les ardents,*' which is in accordance with the view of Wundt.

The idea of a fundamental opposition between the ' *tempérament d'épargne*' and the ' *tempérament de dépense*' has its own appeal. If we make a tentative translation into ' lavish ' and ' economical,' a picture of opposing types is called up. If we permitted to ourselves the use of the conventional term ' psychic energy ' we should explain these conflicting types by saying that the one, the ' *tempérament de dépense,*' spends energy lavishly without reference to the value of the activity, while the other, the ' *tempérament d'épargne,*' gives to each activity the measure which it requires. The same idea is to be found in the popular phrase ' husbanding his resources.' But if, granting that the types so named have significance for us we do not yet wish to make use in explanation of the hypothesis of psychic energy, then we should have to fall back upon such an explanation as would be suggested by Watson's general activity level. We cannot at this stage assume that in respect of this

---

[1] Tempérament et Caractère, pages 1-9.

rate of functioning a definite demarcation can claim to be established, nor can we claim that it could ever be taken as the one fundamental basis of 'types,' but we cannot fail to notice how again and again the widely differing accounts of the writers we have considered have tended to reduce themselves to a classification on the basis of speed of reaction, persistence of reaction. and what we may agree to call the disturbing effect of emotional experience.

It is of passing interest to take note of a point made by Shand as to the conflicting opinions on the nervous temperament. It will be remembered that the nervous was for a time classed as a fifth temperament until with some writers it ousted entirely the melancholic. No agreement seems to have been reached as to whether this belongs to the quick or slow reaction type. In the classifications given in detail above it is clear that the Nervous Temperament is held to connote great vivacity and sensitiveness. J. S. Mill, for example, says :—

'It is what is meant by spirit—People of this temperament are the material of great orators— great preachers—impressive diffusers of moral influences.'[1]   On the other hand Fouillée credits the Nervous Temperament with a slow but intense reaction, and this would seem to be borne out by Dr. N. Ach's recent classification. To the four classical temperaments he adds a fifth, to which he gives the name 'cautious,' and though he does not specify a 'nervous temperament,' it is probable that his melancholic temperament approaches

---

[1] Quoted by Shand. Foundations of Character, page 138.

the most closely to the old nervous temperament, and this (the melancholic) he includes definitely with the slow reaction ones.

The question arises, says Shand, of whether the Nervous Temperament is one of great rapidity of mental action or one in which the characteristics are intensity and prolongation of emotion. This lack of uniformity among writers is obviously prejudicial to a general acceptance of the classical doctrine.

Another point of passing interest in reference to Fouillée's treatment is the fact that he does not abandon the ancient idea of a 'mixed temperament' which shall combine in harmony the characteristics of the four, although such a combination is, in his terminology, rather an equilibrium of the functions of metabolism, and of the activities of the nerves and muscles. He says, for example, ' *Le tempérament complet et harmonieux est l'équilibre d'une intégration suffisament rapide et intense. Quand le système sanguin, le système nerveux et le système musculaire sont également bien constitués et en mutuel accord, on a le tempérament dynamique par excellence. Le tempérament a tout le long de la vie deux grandes influences que l'on ne devrait pas négliger, l'une sur le bonheur, l'autre sur la moralité même.*'[1] He does not, however, make it clear whether he believes in influence of temperament on character to act otherwise, than through the emotions which are presumably the medium of its effect upon happiness.

Reviewing the opinions expressed in this

---

[1] Tempérament et Caractère, pages 80 and 88.

chapter we may perhaps be led to feel that the distinction drawn by Shand between 'temper' and ' temperament ' is not so radical but that they would be reconciled into a single factor, provided it were given a neutral name which would not in itself provoke controversy. It may be that what we are seeking is in some way a temper-temperament combination. We saw that McDougall allowed to the conative aspect of each instinct a specific temper differing in differing individuals. It may be useful to inquire into the exact nature of the differing manifestations which he admits. He holds that ' temper ' which is particularized by such adjectives as ' fiery ', ' fickle,' or ' hopeful,' is not determined by the relative strength of specific instincts. We have seen that according to Mc-Dougall variations in strength of specific instincts constitute in their totality what is known as the ' disposition of an individual.' He believes that ' temper ' is in fact a general quality which pervades, or is apt to pervade, all activities of the individual irrespective of the particular impulse which is aroused. From this he derives his definition of ' temper ' as ' the expression of the way in which the conative impulses work.' In this statement, containing the hypothesis of a general factor of ' temper,' we see a marked contrast to Shand's views in which the ' temper ' is limited to the workings of specific emotions and his corresponding conception of ' temperament ' as the sum of specific ' tempers.' While Shand denies to either term the significance of a unit factor, McDougall believes that each operates essentially in a general manner.

What is of immediate importance for our present inquiry is the lines of action along which McDougall claims that the ' temper ' makes itself felt. ' There are,' he says, ' three principal ways in which the working of the impulses varies from one man to another, namely in respect of (1) strength, intensity or urgency, (2) of persistency and (3) of affectability. By " affectability " I mean the degree to which the impulses are influenced by pleasure and by pain. It seems clear that some men are more liable than others to be checked and diverted from their course of action, and to be prevented from returning to any similar line of action, by the pain of difficulty and thwarting encountered ; and to be more strongly sustained in their striving, and stimulated to further and renewed efforts along similar lines, by the pleasure that comes with progress and success ; the temper of such men is of high affectability.'[1]

A comparison will at once suggest itself between these aspects of the manifestation of 'temper' and the three determinants of ' initial activity level,' ' persistence of original level ' and ' degree of emotionality ' which we have already isolated in a tentative manner from other theories of temperament. The correspondence is not perfect ; ' Affectability' for example in the sense outlined by McDougall cannot be considered synonymous with the factor of ' general emotionality ' which we investigated above; it would seem itself to be allied closely to the question of persistency of effort. The factor of persistency as outlined by McDougall, would,

---

[1] Outline of Psychology, page 353.

however, appear to differ from affectability in being independent of accompanying affect. In reference to this point he writes :—

' It seems equally clear that men differ widely also in respect of the persistency of their impulses and desires and that persistency does not vary with, is not closely correlated with, strength and urgency. There are men whose impulses seem to be very urgent, and who yet show little perseverance . . . On the other hand there are men whose impulses seem to be not very urgent, who are not easily excited to desire and action and yet who, once set upon a goal, hold their course tenaciously or return to it again and again after every diversion. Such persistency can be cultivated in some degree ; but it seems clear that, like urgency and affectability, it is given in the innate constitution of some men in a much higher degree than to others.[2] McDougall holds that the combination of the three factors he has outlined determine the ' temper ' of the individual, and that it is possible to analyse such descriptions as ' fiery,' ' sluggish,' ' obstinate ' into these three quantitative constituents.

At this point it is necessary to remind ourselves that these three differentiating aspects are here being claimed in respect of a general character which is in itself distinguished from ' temperament.' Whether or not we consider McDougall's case for the existence of a general ' temper ' to be well established we must recognize that he is dealing with characters already familiar to us in the discus-

---

[1] Outline of Psychology, page 353.

sion of temperament. But when he himself turns to 'temperament' he gives it the vague and provisional definition we have already noted, viz., 'that it is the sum of the effects upon mental life of the metabolic or chemical changes continually going on in all the tissues of the body.' He assumes that the influence of the chemical substances circulating in the blood acts in part directly upon the nervous system as a whole and in part selectively upon certain centres. He recognizes in this connexion the dominating part played by the endocrine glands, but adds to this the influence of constitutional peculiarities of the nervous system, as for example liability to fatigue. He gives no attempt at classification on this basis but remarks simply that since temperament is the result of so many diverse factors, its varieties are innumerable and cannot be described by means of a few stereotyped terms. It is however interesting to note at this point that McDougall includes in his discussion of temperament the factors of 'introversion' and 'extroversion' familiar in the writings of Jung. The basis on which individuals are divided into two fundamental types—the introvert and the extrovert—will be dealt with in a later chapter, but one point must be made here. We should have found it helpful if McDougall could at this juncture have put forward any theory as to the possible connexion between the functions of introversion and extroversion and the specific nature of any metabolic changes but he merely includes them under the same heading and diagnoses the degree of introversion as an important factor in determining the course of mental development. It may be that McDougall himself feels that there is more in temperament than a vague physiological background provided by metabolic changes and that ultimately, if we are to have a sound classification, it must be on a basis of combined temper and temperament, the possibility of which we have already suggested.

CHAPTER VII

THE FACTORS OF WILL AND PERSEVERATION

THE close association generally maintained between temperament and character is undoubtedly derived chiefly from the emotional factor which we have just discussed. But further connexion is sometimes urged between temperament and what we are accustomed to describe as willed action. The allusions which have been made above to the persistence of reaction as a possible temperamental factor will at once call up a reference to the 'strong and weak willed types'. It may be that if we attempt to analyse what we mean by the strong or the weak will we shall be driven to state the distinction in terms similar to those we have already employed, and that therefore the argument will not progress except in circular fashion. It may also be objected that the scientific treatment of temperamental differences can in no way be advanced by the invocation of an abstract 'Will.' With this objection we shall be in entire agreement. It is customary at this stage of psychology to speak not of the will but rather of volitional action, and to recognise in this not the isolated effect of one abstract 'faculty' but an integrated activity based upon the building up of the self-regarding sentiment. But we find that even in psychological writings the exact connotation of 'willed action' varies greatly. An example of this will appear when we have to consider some contemporary American experimental research into the question of temperament. Such discrepancies have constantly to be born in mind. The question arises here, in view of the great importance of Ach's classification of temperaments which formed part of his wide investigations into the nature of acts of will. The following brief summary of Ach's work is not intended in any sense as a comment upon his theory of will, but simply as the necessary preliminary explanation of his consequent demarcation of temperamental differences.

The results of experiments which he made led him to postulate certain determining tendencies as one aspect of will. In these experiments the determining tendency was constituted by the particular instructions given by the experimenter. To the power of an idea so to determine future action as to make that action accord with itself he gave the name of determining tendency. The perseveration of these tendencies, after working in the subconscious, ensures that the act of will shall be performed according to plan. The importance of these determining tendencies as a factor of willed action is seen clearly in its relation to concentration of attention, and also in the part, which, with association, it plays in the process of abstraction. Ach indeed claims that determined abstraction makes us independent of association since through it the material given by experience can be arranged in new combinations. The existence of these determining tendencies, is, Ach claims, accompanied by an 'awareness of consent.'

To the whole process of energetic decision in so far as it is a purely mental process, Ach gives the name of the 'Primary Will Act.' The total effectiveness of volition has to be considered in reference to the inborn strength of the determining tendencies and to the amount of resistance encountered. The emotional aspect of will is ascribed to the strong feeling produced by a satisfaction of the determining tendency.

Round this theory of willed action Ach has built his classification of the temperaments. His terminology corresponds to a large extent with that of the classical doctrine, but Ach takes no account of the physiological basis on which that doctrine rested. He considers the temperament as an expression of individual differences in feeling and willing capacity and in the general strength of persistence of determining tendencies.

It would appear from his account that he regards these differences largely as innate and he does in fact refer to 'inborn determining tendencies', but he does not make it clear whether he identifies these inborn tendencies with the 'specific instincts' of other writers or with physiological differences of structure or function.

To the four temperaments of the ancient classification he adds a fifth—the cautious—which would appear to hold in Ach's view the same superior position awarded as we have seen by some writers to the 'nervous temperament.'

Thus, the cautious temperament is marked by a high degree of sensitiveness to external stimuli and by strong determining tendencies which are maintained at their original high level throughout the course of the action initiated by them. The sanguine temperament shows an equal degree of sensitiveness and an equally strong initial activity, but in this case the determining tendencies fail to maintain for long duration their original strength. The choleric type, though also possessed of a high degree of sensitiveness is marked by a much lower level of determination and is therefore much less likely to issue in successful action. The phlegmatic temperament is on the other hand distinguished by a low stimulability, but by constantly maintained determination, while at the lowest end of the scale is the melancholic temperament showing at the same time a low level of stimulability and of determination.

It is clear that there are marked discrepancies between the mental characteristics which Ach ascribes to his temperaments and those already enumerated in the earlier attempts to classify under these same terms. Since, however, it is improbable that Ach was concerned with the classical doctrine of the temperaments except in so far as it afforded a familiar terminology to which he could ally the results of his investigations, it would not be profitable to establish a lengthy comparison between the two systems. We may, perhaps, illustrate the discrepancy by contrasting

Ach's description of the choleric subject as marked by a low level of determination, with Richerand's account of the bilious temperament leading to ambitiously conceived and successfully completed action.

From the point of view of the individual the cautious temperament is clearly in all respects the most advantageous, the melancholic is incontestably the greatest handicap. According as the degree of sensitiveness or the maintenance of the initial level of determination is held to be the most valuable factor, the sanguine or the phlegmatic will claim the next position of superiority. The choleric type would appear to be heavily handicapped, but in the accompanying high degree of stimulability to have the germs of possible recompense.

On the basis of Ach's classification we can imagine the temperamental position of an individual indicated graphically by the two co-ordinates—degree of stimulability producing the initial level of reaction, and duration of initial activity level determined by strength of determining tendencies. In the first dimension we see again a factor akin to the initial speed of reaction which has already been isolated from previous theories. The second factor has also appeared before although no attempt has hitherto been made to give an account of its nature. We may feel that Ach's account of 'determining tendencies' has not altogether lifted us out of the obscurity which surrounds willed action. It may seem to us that while the 'determining tendencies' which are set up by definite instructions from the experimentor may be a concrete and intelligible factor, we are on less certain ground when speaking of innate determining tendencies. It was noticed above that a considerable school of modern psychological thought regards volitional action as bound up with what is generally called the integration of the organism and believes that the medium of this integration is the growth of the self regarding sentiment and all that it involves. It might be open to us to regard these sentiments as supplying the 'psychic energy' of the determining tendencies if we were not averse to invoking the adventitious aid which such a concept affords. In any case if we agree to the use of the term 'volitional action' only in this sense of integration it is clear that its effect as seen in ordinary activities must be the result of highly specialised training by experience in life, and could not therefore be regarded as an inborn factor. It would follow that any attempt to investigate the existence of a general temperamental factor colouring all activities must be based on experiments in which the influence of acquired interests and sentiments is reduced to a minimum.

It is recognized by psychologists who endeavour to investigate willed action, that a distinction must be drawn between what is known as 'perseveration' and a special quality of persistence which they attribute to the will.

Thus for Ach the determining tendencies are subject to the influence of 'perseveration' and the perseverating determining tendencies do not, as has been shown, constitute the whole of the activity of the will. This point is emphasized by Dr. Webb. He himself, as the result of his investigations on Character and Intelligence, postulates a factor 'W' which he identifies with persistence of motives, and which appears, he says, to coincide largely with Ach's conception of will.

The question of 'perseveration' as such is attended by a real difficulty since it appears on all the different levels of mental activity. Inasmuch as any experimental investigation of temperament is bound to take account of this factor, and the more descriptive accounts of 'types' also make use of it, it is perhaps advisable to consider what limitations are now attached to the use of the term 'perseveration' in psychology.

The research of Dr. Webb was followed by that of Dr. Lankes whose work on 'Perseveration' was published in 1915. His object was to discover how far the factor of deliberate motive was connected with the intensity of after impressions to which Müller gave the name of 'secondary function.' It might be possible, he conceived, that ideas perseverating unconsciously might be responsible for what appears to be persistence of will. The question which he set himself to investigate was therefore, 'How is perseveration as a peculiarity of the cognitive side of mental life related to perseveration qualities of character?'[1] His experiments were designed to bring out the persistence of the after effects of an experience, and its power to inhibit by unconscious activity the

---

[1] Perseveration. British Journal of Psychology, Vol. VII. Part IV. March 1915, page 388.

G

conscious mental activity of the individual. His conclusion is given in his own words :—'The perseveration tested by the above experiments is a native quality of the nervous system innately different with different individuals. The perseveration tested by qualities of character and behaviour is the result, not of nature and the native system alone, but of that and of the individual's own effort and will. The absence of correlation proves the independence of innate Perseveration and Will and the slightly negative correlations tend to show that the Self... can modify and directly counteract its own nervous system and its innate tendency towards Perseveration or the opposite.'[1] The experimental results encourage he claims, a hopeful outlook in those interested in education and in the real value and possibilities of the human personality.

This conclusion will have to be taken into account in the consideration of those theories of temperament which emphasize 'Perseveration' as one of its factors.

The points of modern psychology which have been raised in this and in the preceding chapter, have made it clear that the difficulties of the consideration of temperament are multiplied exceedingly when an attempt is made to incorporate it into a scientific account of character. Mr. Shand's disintegration of temperament into the tempers of specific emotions, and Ach's theory of the Will introduce elements of a complexity which has not hitherto appeared.

---

[1]British Journal of Psychology. March 1915, pages 418-419.

Such accounts seem to be far removed from the original postulate of a definite physical basis. They appear to deduce the temperaments by splitting up more complex characters rather than to build up a complex system from a simple predicated basis of temperaments.

Therefore we may be inclined to say either that the idea of the temperaments as simple because essentially physical must be wrong, or else that it is impossible to connect immediately a simple doctrine of temperament with a highly complex concept of character.

Let us at this point review again the problem which we set out to investigate and let us weigh against it any progress which we can claim to have made in regard to its solution. We have sought and failed to find a clear-cut scientific and universally accepted definition of the term 'temperament.' We have yet seen evidence in writings extending over a period of more than two thousand years of a belief that behaviour is coloured by a general factor known as temperament. Some believe that this is innate and unmodifiable, others believe that while its constituents may be given at birth they are modifiable by climate, education, or injections, but, that while it is operative its effects are felt in widely different reactions. We have seen evidence of a belief—constant in its essence though varying widely in its basis—that physiological functioning— possibly connected closely with physical structure— produces variation in reaction to environment Such variation we have found to be clearly associated with initial speed of reaction and maintenance of original activity level. But we have also seen that such factors are profoundly affected by degree of emotional disturbance and that if, therefore, evidence can be established for variation in susceptibility to emotional stimuli it must form part of the temperamental equipment.

We use the term 'variation in susceptibility to emotional stimuli' guardedly as a periphrasis under cover of which the controversy as to a factor of 'general emotionality' versus the sum of the tempers of specific emotions may be for the moment ignored.

Modern psychology, investigating distinctions between perseveration of impressions and persistence in a course of action, and between the constituents which go to make up what is known as 'willed action' has introduced elements which complicate the problem. Yet the search for 'types' continues undeterred by the objection that, however complicated may be the classification worked out, the vast majority of men must remain uncatalogued for ever. This objection is in itself an interesting one. It may be said to embody a wide-felt complaint against a tendency to regard classification as a final goal. Even if such classification were comprehensive, yet, it is argued it may be utterly barren since the mere pigeon-holing of individuals does not of necessity advance the cause of human happiness at all. To this it might be replied that the power to predict all reactions of a given individual may have a very definite utilitarian value provided that it could be established upon a satisfactory basis. But this zeal for classification, or at least for loose grouping, must arise from a real fundamental need experienced by the classifiers themselves. One may conjecture that it has its roots in a recognition of the very real difficulties which arise from what is known in common speech as 'incompatibility of temperament.' In the relations of people one to another such incompatibility may prove a real and vital obstacle to profitable intercourse. If the course of man's life is considered as a general process of adaptation to environment then it may well be that his fellow-creatures will constitute the most difficult aspect of the adjustment process. It is then not unnatural that the enquiring mind should seek to determine what are the discernible factors at work in such adjustment, in the hope that if they can be established the worst difficulties may be overcome. The principle which would underlie this belief, would be that resentment against differences would tend to disappear if the nature of the differences could be understood.

On the other hand there is the attitude which, less concerned with the reaction of the individual as a whole, yet strives to dissect his various activities into compartments which do not overlap, in the hope that the sum of such dissections will on being reassembled, again constitute the complete individual. Such an attitude has already been touched upon, and it has been recognized that there is a danger of losing the unified living principle which we prefer to believe is the real individual. It is attacked most vigorously by those who emphasize what they call the dynamic aspect of life, and who can claim that the individual must be treated as a whole, as a unit centre of living activity. What we may call for the moment the dissection as opposed to the dynamic school reply that whatever truth may lie in this attack it is yet only by the process of separating out, that the activities of living beings can hope to be brought under scientific investigation.

What immediately concerns us at the moment is that, as the result of this fundamental difference in attitude, there will be a corresponding difference in the types of classification evolved. The dynamic school, treating men as a whole will produce a broad general scheme. The prototype of such a classification will be found in the 'Psychological Types' of Jung. On the other hand the 'dissectional' school will confine itself, or will seek to do so, to certain more or less isolated aspects. It is customary to allude to these aspects as traits of 'personality,' the term personality being introduced in order to avoid the complexities of character and the historical impediments of 'temperament.' Certain American experiments may be taken as a good example of this system of investigation. We must now consider in detail the results of each method of attack and will begin with the more general scheme outlined in Jung's 'Psychological Types.'

CHAPTER VIII

TEMPERAMENT AND ANALYTICAL PSYCHOLOGY

IN his introductory chapter to 'Psychological Types' Jung defines the motive which inspires his work in these words :—

'It is my hope that this insight may prove a clarifying contribution to a dilemma which, not in analytical psychology alone, but in other provinces of science and particularly in the personal relations of human beings to one another, has led to misunderstanding and divisions. For it explains how the existence of two distinct types is actually a fact which has long been known. Notwithstanding the diversity of formulations the common basis or fundamental idea shines constantly through, viz., in the one case an outward movement of interest towards the object and in the other a movement of interest away from the object towards the subject and his own psychological processes.'[1]

The question at issue from our point of view is whether the important doctrine which he formulates can be connected at any point with an attempt to classify, according to temperament, in whatever way it may be defined. It may perhaps be best to

---

[1] Psychological Types, page 11.

begin with a bald statement of the nature of the types which he describes. The terms 'Introvert' and 'Extrovert' in terms of which he makes his great distinction, suggest in themselves the point of view from which the distinction is made. He further differentiates according to the four basal functions—thinking—feeling—sensation—intuition, so that he recognizes in all eight distinct types, viz.,

Extroverted Thinking Extroverted Feeling	} extroverted rational
Extroverted Sensation Extroverted Intuitive	} extroverted irrational
Introverted Thinking Introverted Feeling	} introverted rational
Introverted Sensation Introverted Intuitive	} introverted irrational

The characteristics appertaining to each of these types may be briefly summarised as follows :—

The direction of the Libido decides the introverted or extroverted nature of the attitude, while the most differentiated function decides the nature of the adaptation. The universal distribution of types has resulted from the ancient biological relation of subject to object. In this relation two alternative solutions were possible—(1) increased

fertility with small degree of defensive power—or
(2) an individual equipment of self protection.
Of these the first has its counterpart in the extroverted attitude—the second corresponds to the
attitude of introversion. Since the determining
factor can no longer be the struggle for existence,
it must be looked for in the disposition of the
child. Jung himself is prepared to admit the
probable importance of physiological factors yet
to be determined. 'In the last analysis' he says,
'it may well be that physiological causes inacces-
sible to our knowledge play a part in this.
Certainly a reversal of type often proves exceedingly
harmful to the physiological well-being of the
organism.'[1]

For the typical extrovert, interest and attention
are fastened upon objective happenings, and the
moral laws approved by society suffice to guide
his actions. The conscious personality is always
the expression of the superior function, but in
the compensatory region of the unconscious, the
inferior functions reveal a subjective and ego-
centric attitude.

THINKING EXTROVERT

In the type of Thinking Extravert the obsession
with objective data results in a comparative lack
of freedom, and in an accumulation of material
acquired empirically from individual experience.
The formula becomes a universal law to which no
exception can be tolerated and consequently this

---

[1] Psychological Types, page 416.

leads to a repression of the activities of feeling. As the rule of the formula makes the conscious life more and more impersonal, so the unconscious becomes more highly sensitive and the resulting disturbance of the unconscious may culminate in a neurosis.

FEELING EXTROVERT

In the extreme case of this type the subject becomes so swallowed up in individual feeling processes that it seems as if there were no longer a subject of feeling but merely a feeling process. The type is chiefly to be found among women, and in its most harmonious representation it is so adjusted to conscious control that the objects of feeling are always the conventionally approved. In this type, thinking, as the function most incompatible with feeling is repressed. There is developed an unconscious compensatory thought, but in the event of what Jung calls a 'dissociation of the personality' the unconscious thinking may give rise to a neurosis of the hysteria variety.

EXTROVERT SENSATION

The extrovert sensation type is pre-eminently realistic. It is chiefly found among men; their aim is concrete enjoyment and morality is similarly orientated. It is accompanied by conspicuously good adjustment to reality and by a great appreciation of style.

EXTROVERT INTUITIVE

The mark of the intuitive extrovert is that he builds into the object as much as he takes out of it. The possibilities opened up to the intuitive type are very wide, and the individual of this type has generally a flair for the new and promising and a dislike of tradition or of stable conditions. It is generally considered to be the most important social type and to have great power of inspiring enthusiasm, provided that the necessary repression of sensations does not lead to a disturbance of the unconscious.

INTROVERTED TYPES

'The Introvert,' says Jung, 'interposes a subjective view between perception of the object and his own action.'[1] The sense in which he defines the subjective factor is 'that psychological action or reaction which when merged with the effect of the object makes a new psychic fact.' Disturbance arises when the ego which Jung defines as the 'focal point of consciousness' tries to usurp the claims of the subject or real self.

THINKING INTROVERT

In this type since thinking begins in the subject and returns to the subject, facts are valued simply as an example of a theory and not for their own sake. The abstract expression which fits the facts is first created, and carries with it a great force of conviction. The influence of this type on others is often repelling and cold, and there is usually a great dislike of publicity. While extremely conscientious in the details of his work the type shows little consideration for the feelings of others. In an extreme case the conviction is rigid and un-

---

[1] Psychological Types, page, 471.

bending, and there is a danger that subjective truth may be confused with the man's own person.

INTROVERTED FEELING TYPE

The intensity of feeling common to this type does not appear on the surface, and is often marked by an air of indifference. The type corresponds largely, Jung suggests, to the old melancholic temperament. The outward demeanour is harmonious and sympathetic, not seeking to impose an attitude on those around. It is a type commonly misunderstood and not credited with feeling. When the type is so extreme that a neurosis ensues, it is accompanied by a suspicious attitude.

INTROVERTED SENSATION TYPE

'This type,' says Jung, 'concerns itself with the subjective percept released by the objective stimulus. Introverted sensation conveys an image whose effect is not so much to reproduce the object as to throw over it a wrapping whose lustre is derived from age old subjective experience and the still unborn future event.'[1]

'Relatively speaking, the type has only archaic possibilities of expression, . . . he moves in a mythological world. . . . As a rule the individual acquiesces in his isolation and in the banality of the reality.'[2]

INTROVERTED INTUITIVE TYPE

This type is equally with the sensation type

---

[1] Psychological Types, page 500.
[2] Ibid., page 503.

difficult of direct apprehension. In Jung's own words 'The introverted intuitive moves from image to image without establishing any connexion between the phenomenon and himself. .... . Since these images represent possible ways of viewing life which in given circumstances have the power to provide a new energetic potential this function is as indispensable to the total psychic economy as is the corresponding human type to the psychic life of a people.'[1]

'A very slight differentiation of judgment transfers intuitive perception from the purely æsthetic to the moral sphere ; the moral intuitive concerns himself with the meaning of the vision.'[2]

Jung himself admits that the two last types are very difficult to distinguish from external signs since nothing is visible except reserve and general uncertainty.

In common with the supporters of the classical doctrine of the temperaments, Jung agrees that the pure type is rarely to be found. This, he ascribes to the existence, side by side with the primary function, of a secondary or inferior function which cannot be of a nature directly opposed to that of the leading function, but which serves to modify its manifestations by conscious or unconscious influence.

In the description of his 'types' Jung sometimes refers to them as 'temperaments' as for example when he says 'The temperament that prefers concrete thinking and grants it substantiality is

---

[1] Psychological Types, page 507.
[2] Ibid., page 509.

distinguished therefore by a preponderance of sense-conditioned representations as against active apperception which springs from a subjective act of will whose aim it is to command the sense-determined representations in accordance with the tendencies of an idea. '[1]

Further he refers to other classifications of the temperaments which show, he believes, some analogy with his own. One of these references is to the work of Furneaux Jordan who in his book on Anatomy and Physiology in Character (1886) distinguishes a shrewish—intermediate—and non-shrewish type—showing some affinity with the introvert and extrovert. Jordan's types are conceived in terms of nerve action. He says, for example, 'The peculiarities of the individual, the party, the faith, the race lie hidden in nerve substance. When nerve failings have been strengthened and nerve overflow checked, nerve proclivities have still to be reckoned with. If character is for the most part a physiological product it follows that education is mainly a physiological art.'[2]

More important is the reference which Jung makes to the work of Ostwald who in his work 'Grosse Männer' compares his two types (the classic and the romantic) with the four classical temperaments with special reference to the peculiarity of slow or rapid actions.

'The slow reaction corresponds with the phlegmatic and melancholic temperaments, the quick reaction with the sanguine and choleric. He

---

[1] Psychological Types, page 376.
[2] Anatomy and Physiology in Character, pages 6-11.

regards the sanguine and phlegmatic as normal middle types, whereas the choleric and melancholic seem to him to be morbid exaggerations of the basic character.'[1]

'This observation of Ostwald's seems entirely convincing since the four antique temperaments were most probably constructed from the same principle as that upon which Ostwald has also established the classic and romantic types. The four temperaments are differentiated from the standpoint of affectivity, i.e., manifest affective reactions. The classification is superficial from the psychological standpoint for it judges exclusively from outward appearance. According to the ancient division the man whose behaviour is outwardly peaceful and inconspicuous belongs to the phlegmatic temperament. He passes as phlegmatic but on the contrary he may be a deeply sensitive, even passionate, nature in whom emotion pursues the inward course.'[2]

So again, as by Shand, the classical doctrine is dismissed as superficial and inadequate, but not this time because it assumes the carrying over of a characteristic from one emotion to another, but rather because it ignores the workings of the unconscious mind and its native orientation.

The foregoing account of Jung's theory may not appear to have made all things clear on this matter of differentiation of types. Certain points, however, stand out as the result of its consideration. The first is, that if we were tempted to make use again

---

[1] Psychological Types, page 403.
[2] Ibid., page 404.

of the analogy of psychic energy, we could say, that Jung's classification is determined primarily by the direction which such energy tends to take spontaneously. In this respect we may contrast it with Berman's 'Endocrine Personalities' in which the determining factors stated in similar terms would be the strength and continuity of flow of such energy. It would also appear that Jung himself felt that the initial division, though fundamental, was inadequate and that to meet this difficulty he introduced the four 'functions' of Thinking, Feeling, Sensation and Intuition. It is sometimes brought forward as a criticism of Jung's doctrine that by this introduction of distinct 'functions' he has reverted to the old 'faculty' psychology and that therefore his method loses its dynamic value and approximates too closely to the dissection mode of attack. But it would be a mistake to conclude that this brings it more into line with other methods of investigation of personality traits which we have yet to describe. It yet remains true that Jung's classification is essentially an abstract one based upon a speculative hypothesis.

He postulates for example the existence side by side of three ranks of functions—the superior which is the chief conscious determinate, the inferior also conscious and which while not incompatible with the superior yet exercises a modifying influence upon it, and finally a compensation function in the unconscious which is often most directly opposed to the primary conscious function and which, if of sufficient strength, may lead to serious dissociation and conflict. Such a hypothesis may appear to be borne out by scientifically observed facts of behaviour but inasmuch as it is unrelated to more familiar psychological knowledge it must obviously be considered by itself, and however valuable the contribution which it makes to the delineation of types, it remains a classification apart.

Reading through Jung's own description of the eight types which he distinguishes we do not find there any such easily drawn picture into which we can put the individuals we know, as we recognized, for example, in Richerand's delineations of temperamental types. At the same time we feel that the insight and erudition which Jung's distinctions indicate are probably more in harmony with psychological truth if such is to be found. As regards the initial and fundamental distinctions of the introvert and extrovert types most people will agree that it corresponds to an observable difference in individuals. This admission is not infrequently qualified by the counter claim that the pure extravert and pure introvert do not exist. There would appear to be a real danger in using the terms introvert and extrovert too much as substantives and too little as verbs. The tendency in modern psychology is, as we have realized, to avoid the pitfalls of hypostatization by speaking rather of functions than of entities.

We have seen that Jung himself further differentiates into what he calls the four primary functions and that his linking of each with extroversion and introversion is based essentially on the question of direction of activity.

H

Comparisons have been drawn between the Psychological Types of Jung and the classical Temperaments. This analogy, which cannot however be deeply stressed, or looked upon as conclusive, would be based upon the standpoint of directed effort. Judged by the standard of Outward or Inward activity, it would appear that the sanguine temperament would find a counterpart in the extroverted type in its purest manifestation, while the melancholic or the alternative 'nervous' temperament would correspond to the pronounced introvert. The old 'choleric' temperament on the other hand would appear to be capable of both great outwardly and great inwardly directed activity while conversely the phlegmatic produces little activity in either direction.

Again, in applying the test of weak or strong general emotionality the choleric and melancholic would appear to be marked by strong feeling, which in the case of the choleric is allowed free activity but in the case of the melancholic is strongly inhibited. On the other hand the phlegmatic and the sanguine show little emotionality and of these the phlegmatic shows a tendency to inhibition which is not present in the sanguine. The effects of this inhibition when it occurs must be looked for in Jung's compensatory function of the unconscious which he describes as the individual accompaniment of each of his types. Such a comparison refers only to the direction taken by the effort and not to the persistency of determining tendencies which was seen to be the chief mark of Ach's classification. A complete doctrine of the temperaments would have to take into account both these factors and would also have to determine what relation exists between the degree of stimulability which Ach makes one of his distinguishing features and the degree of Outward or Inward activity described by Jung.

It will be remembered that Jung believed that the clue to the differentiation must be sought in the disposition of the child, and that he further admitted that in the last result the determining factor might prove to be physiological. In seeking any such physiological connexion we should naturally turn to the latest embodiment in the endocrine theory. We might attempt, for example, to draw a superficial parallel between Berman's principal gland types and the primary functions of Jung. Thus a correspondence may conceivably be found to exist between the types.

> Ante Pituitary and Thinking Function.
> Post Pituitary and Feeling Function.
> Thyroid and Intuitive Function.
> Adrenal and Sensation Function.

As to the differences of orientation towards the object or towards the subject, which Jung holds to be rooted in biological necessity, there is in Berman's doctrine no clue as to any secretion determinant.

This comparison does not obviously take us very far and it will be more profitable to turn to the distinction drawn in Chapter IV between the conditions known respectively as vagotonia and sympatheticotonia. It will be remembered that

these terms were used to denote excessive irritability in respect of the sympathetic and
parasympathetic systems of which the actions
are mutually antagonistic. It was further seen that
an active thyroid suprarenal system was closely
allied with the condition of sympatheticotonia and
with a rapid response to the demands of the external
world. It might then be not unreasonable to
suppose that the function of extroversion is linked
up with the sympatheticotonic condition, that is
with an active thyroid suprarenal system. No
such direct evidence can be brought forward in
support of an alliance between vagotonia and
introversion. On the other hand it might be
conjectured that the less harmoniously the thyroid
and suprarenal systems work together the more
likely is the tendency to introversion. All this is
pure conjecture and too much importance must
not be attached to it, but there should arise a hope
that if Jung is right in his distinction and that if
the endocrine workers on the other hand are right
in the profound effects which they ascribe to the
endocrine functions, then a relation between the
two should in time emerge.

It is easier to see a connection between Jung's
doctrine and the Freudian theory of conflict between
what he calls the pleasure-pain and the reality
principles. Such conflict is essentially between the
group of sex instincts—using the term 'sex' in its
widest connotation—and the 'ego' instincts. Of
these the sex instincts, occupied essentially with the
perpetuation of the race, have a corresponding
outward tendency to which the function of extro-

version would appear to afford a parallel. The ego instincts on the other hand, concerned chiefly with the development, and maintenance intact, of the owner's individuality may in their turn be served most usefully by the function of introversion. There is here an attractive and valuable link between two great theories. It affords no clue to a possible physiological basis other than the instinct neurograms in which these permeating influences inherited at birth are supposed to be housed. The analogy is worked out clearly in Miller's 'Types of Mind and Body.' It is there suggested that the conflict between these two fundamental instincts is determined by what are termed 'endocrine habits,' that is, a tendency towards the production of metabolic processes, which lay down a somatic substratum on which future reactions are built. All differences in character are looked upon as essentially based upon this differentiation between two fundamental instinctive drives. Miller admits the justification for Jung's major division but complains of the loss of dynamic unity produced by the further division into functions, and prefers the fundamental division into Cyclothymes and Schizothymes.

This distinction was evolved from the investigation of psychiatrists and is associated in particular with the work of Kretschmer. Character according to Kretschner consists in the mass of affective and volitional reactive possibilities of an individual, but the basis of temperament he ascribes to the working of the cerebro-glandular apparatus.

He distinguishes from the point of view of phy-

sique between the pyknic and asthenic types. The
pyknic type corresponds with the thickset somewhat
stumpy physique, the asthenic to the tall and lean.
A similar divergence is outlined on the psychological
plane between the cyclothymic and schizothymic
types. Between the two but inclining more to the
cyclothymic is the syntonic, which is accepted as the
normal. The cyclothymic, as the name suggests,
implies a moderately easy adaptation to the requirements of the external world, and corresponds
roughly to the extrovert delineated by Jung. In
the schizothymic on the other hand, there is an
approximate splitting of the personality, some
difficulty in adjustment to reality and a consequent
tendency towards introverted activity.

Roback in his comprehensive historical treatment
of the psychology of character criticizes the lack
of fundamental principles in such classifications as
those of Kretschmer. This raises again the very
important issue of the most profitable line of
attack. He claims that any investigation of
character must be based upon the belief that
inhibition is the primary function in the growth of
character, but in the matter of temperament, the
object of our immediate investigation, he is less
definite. He contents himself with the warning
that the term temperament should be reserved
for the affective side of personality. He draws
attention to the 'bewildering labyrinth of theories'
which the history of the study of temperament
discloses and concludes that 'our knowledge of
the temperaments has advanced even if we do
not appreciate the gain.'

'Before the psychological attack, armed with the munition of endocrinology, could be successful—and this seems to be the destiny of the study from present indications—it was necessary for the other theories to serve as scientific fodder. Some of these have gone to become the flesh and blood of more vigorous doctrines ; others have once for all been cast off as refuse, but even these latter have their historical value. It is interesting in this historical light to note how a certain theory keeps cropping up again and again throughout the ages in an increasingly modern form. The common element in many theories is of even greater significance. A critical tendency in all the listed theories could be discovered, although it would be far from reasonable to affirm that this critical tendency represents more nearly the truth than some isolated points of view latterly held.'[1]

Roback is however more interested in the building up of a science of character than in the elucidation of a temperamental factor if such may be shown to exist. In the final chapters of his books—devoted to his constructive hypothesis of the basis of character—he gives some attention to the relation of temperament and character but he is content in this connection to use the old classification of sanguine—choleric—melancholic and phlegmatic and the vaguely descriptive qualities applied to each. We cannot dispute that the study of temperament must always serve as a handmaid to the study of character, and it may appear that our search for a

---

[1] Psychology of Character, page 108.

temperamental factor indicates a pursuit of what is only a side issue. But our contention is rather that the elucidation of this factor of temperament— the name of which as we have seen occurs repeatedly in the literature of every age—even if it should eventually lead to the denial of its functions—is in itself a necessary preliminary to any scientific treatment of the concept of character. In adopting this attitude we must risk the accusations of replacing the dynamic by the static conception— and of concentrating upon isolated elements rather than upon a functioning whole.

CHAPTER IX

CONTEMPORARY RESEARCH INTO
THE ANALYSIS OF PERSONALITY

I F we turn now to those psychologists who seek
to investigate experimentally 'personality, 'but
who attack it rather from the angle of discrete
manifestations than from that of a dynamic unity,
we find that here too there is a tendency to emphasize
two different aspects which seem at the moment
likely to establish a distinct cleavage in the method
of attack of the subject. These two aspects may
be differentiated according as they emphasize the
emotional side on the one hand and on the other
the conative element which is bound up with the
will. Evidence of these different methods of attack
must be sought primarily in the work of contemporary American psychologists.

In the 'Guide to the Descriptive Study of the
Personality' published by Messrs. Augustus Hoch
and Georges Amsden in the review of Neurology
and Psychiatry (XI), it is laid down that the
affective reactions of the individual are of
greatest importance, and have a significant
bearing upon the total output of energy. An
attempt is made to form a complete estimate

of the subject's personality under the following heads—

    i.   Traits relating to the Intelligence.
    ii.   Output of Energy.
    iii.   Subject's estimate of himself.
    iv.   Adaptability towards Environment.
    v.   Mood.
    vi.   Instinctive Tendencies.
    vii.   General Interests.
    viii.   Pathological Traits.

Under the fifth heading of 'Moods' the writers base their questions upon the characteristics of the four classical temperaments emphasizing the aspects of continuity of reaction to pleasure. 'Adaptability towards Environment' covers the attitude towards reality and direction of activities. It may be supposed that Groups IV, V, and VI, together with II, would form the writer's conception of 'temperament' in its rôle in personality.

We may contrast this account with that of Miss June Downey's investigation of what she calls the 'Will Temperament.' She lays down the instinctive, the emotional, and the temperamental as distinct features of individual equipment.

The estimation of the varying strength of different specific instincts, of the level of energy, and of emotional susceptibility are the fundamental requirements in her estimate of personality. Power of inhibition and nervous stability are the balancing factors between the abnormal and the normal, and combined with the rapidity of reaction constitute the criteria which determine the 'types' of personality. So for example James's types of the

Explosive and the Obstructed Will arise from the relative superiority of impulsion or inhibition.

The object of her present scheme of Will-Temperament tests, is given as to 'test out activity or the dynamic level of personality.' Muscular movements and their inhibitions are held to reveal temperament, to which she ascribes an intellectual, instinctive and emotional aspect, and the particular form of muscular movement which she investigates is that of handwriting executed under given conditions. For example writing under distraction of attention will bring out the explosive type or the controlled type. The temperamental pattern of the individual is held to be determined by two factors :—

(i) the amount of nervous energy at the disposal of the individual,

(ii) the tendency of such nervous energy to discharge immediately into the motor area that innervates the muscles and glands, or to find a way out by a roundabout pathway of discharge.

A tendency to hyperkinetic discharge may result from either a high level of activity or from a great simplification of pathways, while a hypokinetic or inhibitive tendency may be due to a low level of activity or to an undue elaboration of impulses. The Will-Temperament test claims to measure innate tendencies, but not emotional reactions, to determine the form assumed by character, but not its content. The essential phases of the dynamic pattern are given as :—

  (i)   the speed and fluidity of reaction
  (ii) the forcefulness and purpose of reaction
  (iii) the carefulness and persistence of reaction.

The corresponding tests are grouped under the headings :—

  (i)   Speed
  (ii) Aggressiveness
  (iii) Persistence

The speed group tests include the determination of what is called 'freedom from load' together with the speed of movement and of decision; 'aggressiveness' includes motor impulsion, resistance to opposition, and finality of judgment. The 'persistence' tests distinguish between interest in detail, co-ordination of impulses, and volitional perseveration.

According as the emphasis of the results falls on the speed, aggressiveness or persistence factor the individual under examination is characterised as mobile, forceful, or deliberate. The graph representing these results is called the will-profile of the individual. The term 'mental set' is used to denote those deep-seated tendencies of the individual which determine the focusing of effort and the direction of attention, and which should be brought to light by the will-temperament tests.

'volitional perseveration' is here considered as a unity divorced from the mere persistence of stimuli or of ideas. It is held to measure 'psychic momentum' which is defined as 'a self-directing activity motivated by inner compulsion.'

Interesting light is thrown by the tests on the

question of possible modification of temperamental factors. It is found that the Will-Profile of the individual varies from year to year and that it tends to become more highly patterned as maturity is reached. ' The setting of a pattern is the symptom of temperamental maturity. '[1] It is not, however, decided whether this change is the result of training and of the formation of specific habits, or a mere natural process of growth. It is suggested that a definitely patterned Will-Profile generalises a particular kind of training which has played into native tendencies. On the whole it is considered probable that the different stages of physiological growth carry with them their own temperamental modifications.

' If different temperamental traits ripen at different physiological ages and so appear at different epochs of development, modifications of temperament are certain to be anticipated. The seven ages of man leave their imprint upon temperament as well as upon the body and moreover temporary physiological conditions must have some effect on temperamental reaction. '[2]

A consideration of Miss Downey's research in conjunction with preceding accounts at once raises certain controversial issues. It may perhaps be advisable to consider these points before attempting to decide the nature of the contribution which the theory makes to our own investigations. The first of these points must, in view of what was said in the last chapter, be the particular function ascribed to the will.

---

[1] Will, Temperament and its Testing, page 256.
[2] Ibid, page 333.

The consideration of the 'Will-Temperament' profile as described in the researches of Miss Downey shows that in this view the idea of the will is identified with the habitual manner of carrying over purpose into action rather than with the development and integration of the organism through the instinct of self-assertion. Further it appears that this carrying over of purpose into action is determined by the amount and speed of flow of the psychic energy available and controlled by the power of inhibition. So the experiments fall entirely within the field of 'level of energy' which in the introduction was described as one of the three requirements in the estimate of personality. The other two were given as the relative strength of specific instincts, and the degree of emotional susceptibility. Of these, the first may be taken to constitute the 'dispositon' of the individual in the narrower sense defined above. 'Personality' then appears to be composed of 'disposition' 'temperament' in the sense of 'energy level' and 'emotional susceptibility.' So the divorce of temperament from emotion would be emphasized, and a further complication would be the consequent divorce of energy and emotion. If temperament is bound up with the output of psychic energy, so also is 'emotion.' If this distinction is pressed, and emotion is regarded simply as the feeling aspect of an instinct, then it will belong to the category of 'disposition' and temperament will be limited exclusively to the conative aspect of behaviour.

The research of Miss Downey invites a comparison

with the results obtained by Ach and given above. Her investigation of the level of energy and its tendency to discharge may be compared with Ach's 'determining tendencies.' Her factors of speed, aggressiveness, and resistance, appear to have a close correspondence with his investigation of will. She, also, speaks of volitional perseveration and emphasises the importance of the amount of resistance which can be overcome.

It is clear, however, that the aspects of personality investigated by Miss Downey, are much more complex than the concentrated essence of will which formed the subject of Ach's experiments. It is difficult to feel that a limitation of the field of temperament has been brought appreciably nearer by her conclusions, while at the same time it is impossible not to realize the validity of the 'types of personality' which she claims to have established. In this connection it is interesting to contrast her statement that the Will Temperament test is a test not of emotional reactions but of innate tendencies with the account given by her of the researches of Allport and Allport on the classification and measurement of personality traits. They, it appears, divide the temperamental aspect of personality into two divisions distinguished respectively as emotional breadth and emotional strength. In their account self expression forms another component of personality and under this category is considered, among other characteristics, the predominance of introversion or extroversion, and they point out that in their investigations the emphasis is on the force of activity rather than upon its direction.

In a general account of the empirical investigations of American experimenters into problems allied to the conception of personality, Roback in his Psychology of Character makes the general criticism that their investigations are inclined to be promiscuous and not backed up by discussion of underlying theory. As to how far the value of their results is on this account depreciated we are not in a position to say. When, if ever, the scientific handling of the concept or character is achieved, it is probable that their researches will be subjected to further analysis and will occupy a valuable place in a general scheme. In spite of protests against the attempt to split up—and pigeon hole aspects of behaviour of which the essential feature is unity, it is doubtful whether by any other means a scientific account can be achieved. It will be in the putting together again of the components that the real test will emerge. In this connexion it is to be observed that the supporters of the behaviourist doctrine—to which the term mechanistic is applied in derogatory sense—claim on behalf of this attitude that the consideration of the behaviour of the individual as a whole, so far from suffering from their method of attack preserves an even greater unity by reduction to certain simple and well defined elements.

In our search for a simplified doctrine of temperament we may then turn hopefully to the writings of the behaviourist school. The results are discouraging but instructive.

CHAPTER X

INDICATIONS FROM THE BEHAVIOURIST DOCTRINE

THE position taken up by the Behaviourist school of psychologists in reference to the existence or function of temperament is uncompromising. 'I wish to draw the conclusion,' says Mr. J. B. Watson, 'that there is no such thing as an inheritance of capacity, habit, temperament, mental constitution and characteristics.'[1] We may be inclined hopefully to imagine, that it is the question of inheritance which he stresses and that to the later activities of the individual as a whole he might allow a temperamental colouring, but we can find no evidence in his writings to give support to this view. It is unnecessary to enter into a detailed account of his theories supporting the view that the whole of human activity consists in conditioned reactions based on a few unlearned responses which, so far as he has been able to discover, are present at birth or can be spontaneously evoked shortly afterwards. The concept of personality cannot, he claims, be understood otherwise than as the reflection of the 'genetic history' of

---

[1]Behaviourism, page 74.

I

our habits. These habits are distinguished in turn as manual, vocal and visceral.

It is in connection with the visceral habits of man that we must look for the root of emotional life. Watson postulates only three primary emotions —fear, rage and love, and to each he gives a small list of definite stimuli which will call forth those spontaneous responses which are commonly said to exhibit these, emotions. These and the list for each emotion is strictly circumscribed—are the only unconditioned stimuli which will call forth the emotional response. For the rest of our life we respond only to stimuli which are conditioned substitutes for the original. It may be advisable at this juncture to study rather more in detail the actual connexion laid down by the behaviourist between visceral stimuli and general bodily reactions and between the whole question of habit organization, and those individual differences in behaviour which we are apt to consider the result, in part at least, of temperamental equipment. There is in the behaviourist theory a fascinating simplicity and in its technique an attractive exactness which must appeal to those who wish to see the science of psychology established on a basis comparable to that of the physical sciences. If, on reading the behaviourist treatises we find, mixed with our admiration of their approach, a wistful feeling that half our difficulties are left unsolved, there is none the less present the recognition that it is on these objective and logical principles, invoking no superfluous concepts, that we should like to leave the issue. Distrust as to the simplicity of the method as at present sketched cannot destroy the sympathy with its line of attack and the hope of further enlightenment.

We may perhaps first call attention to Watson's preliminary statement that the changing pressure in the visceral organs gives rise to visceral stimuli which in turn evoke responses not only of the organ in question, but of the whole body It is because of the vague reactions of the whole body to which visceral stimuli may give rise that Watson ascribes the increasingly important rôle which the viscera are now playing in psycological theory. We should then expect that the behaviourist will look to the visceral stimuli and reactions for the key to that which we speak of familiarly as emotional disturbance. In point of fact, the behaviourist school as expounded by Watson maintains that all so called emotional experiences can be accounted for on the theory of conditioned stimulus and response ; and that they can be studied by the same mechanism as that available for investigation of simple reflex action. We have seen elsewhere that Watson allows for three 'emotional reactions' —fear, rage and love which can apparently be called forth in a very young child by certain definite stimuli. Such reactions he would call unconditioned. He denies that in accepting this doctrine, any such specific theory of the emotions as that propounded by James is required. His conclusion, in his own words is as follows—'The main point to emphasize here is that practically every responding organ of the body can be conditioned ; and that this conditioning takes place not only throughout adult life, but can and does take place daily from the moment of birth (in all probability before birth). Most of this organization takes place below the verbalized level. Indeed the glands and unstriped muscular tissues do not belong to our so called voluntary system of responses at all. . . . ' . . . The importance of early conditionings in building up bodily attitudes, especially on the emotional side, is almost undreamed of. It is practically impossible for us in adult life to have a "new" stimulus thrust upon us that does not arouse vestigial organization. This work helps us too in understanding why behaviourists are growing away from the concept of instinct and substituting for it bodily sets and attitudes.'[1]

In dealing with the part played by specific endocrine glands, Watson contents himself for the most part with outlining the definite physiological effects occurring from the over or under activity of the particular gland in question. These effects have already been stated in bare outline in Chapter IV. He does, however, refer to 'emotional excitement' and the accompanying release of increased supplies of adrenin. So far, all that Watson has to say is in direct accord with the physiological doctrine agreed upon as the result of far reaching experimental investigation. The particular contribution which the behavourist has to make to the problem is in the possibility of a conditioned response relationship in respect of the endocrine glands. Watson admits that there is as yet no

---

[1]Behaviourism, page 34.

sure evidence to show that the activity of the endocrine glands can be conditioned. In view of the acknowledged importance of the rôle played by the ductless glands in general development there is, he says, urgent need to investigate the possibility of conditioning in their regard. He himself believes strongly that these reactions can be conditioned.

'We know,' he writes, 'that unconditioned stimuli arousing the reactions we call fear and rage bring about an increase of adrenin. We now know that fear and rage behaviour can be conditioned. We have some reason now to think that the thyroid is directly thrown into activity by unconditioned sex stimuli and since we know that positive sex behaviour can be conditioned we have good theoretical grounds for holding that thyroid activity can be conditioned. The evidence is fair for holding that in the whole bodily process we call conditioning the ductless glands are intimately involved—that conditioned stimuli may bring about both over secretion (hyperactivity) and under secretion (hyposecretion) of the ductless glands.'[1] If these theories should prove eventually to be justified, and if ever the conditioning of responses in respect of the ductless glands is worked out in scientific detail, then such reactions might be said to constitute the temperamental determinant of individual behaviour and the importance of conditioning in the life of the very young child would be at once apparent.

On the subject of individual differences the

---

[1] Behaviourism, page 69.

behavourist contention is, that, apart from the individual variations in structure, there is no evidence of variation in individual response. We have seen that what he calls man's 'unlearned repertoire of acts' is in his view extremely circum-scribed. The rest is habit formation and he adds the rider that 'habit formation starts in all probability in embryonic life and that even in the human young environment shapes behaviour so quickly that all of the older ideas about what types of behaviour are inherited and what are learned, break down. Grant variations in structure at birth, and rapid habit formation from birth, and you have here a basis for explaining many of the so called facts of inheritance of "mental" characteristics.'[1] Watson supports this statement by the claim that given any healthy infant at birth and full power to control its environment it is possible to fashion any ultimate product which may be desired. As a corollary he postulates that the concept of instinct has become unnecessary. For the acts which appear spontaneously and for which no learned habit formation can be found to account, he gives the explanation that given the body of the human being, constituted in its own particular fashion any other reactions would, on chemical and physical grounds, be impossible. In addition he makes the claim that habit formation begins from the earliest moment of the child's life and that therefore by the time the so-called 'instincts' of psychology are supposed to manifest

---

[1] Behaviourism, page 79.

themselves the child is already a 'graduate student in the subject of learned responses.'

Turning next to the question of emotion, he finds, as the result of observation of infants under a controlled environment, only three unlearned emotional pattern reactions. The rest of the complicated reactions which we are prone to describe as emotional have, he claims, been built in round these three unconditioned patterns by simple habit formation based upon the substitution of stimulus or response. We need not give in detail the experimental evidence which Watson brings forward in support of this view Two points are, however, relevant to our discussion. The first, for which we are already prepared, is that while overt actions are present to some extent in all emotional states, yet the predominant factor is undoubtedly a visceral one. On this Watson bases a claim which would appear to be a significant one and which, substantiated, must have a profound effect upon modern psychology. 'I want,' he writes, 'to develop the thesis that society has never been able to get hold of these implicit concealed visceral and glandular reactions of ours, or else it would have schooled them in us. Hence most of our adult overt reactions—our speech, the movements of our arms, legs and trunk, are schooled and habitised. Owing to their concealed nature, however, society cannot get hold of visceral behaviour to lay down rules and regulations for its integration. It follows as a corollary from this that we have no means, no words with which to describe these reactions. They remain unverbalised . . . Because then of the fact that we have never verbalised these responses, a good many things happen to us that we cannot talk about. We have never learned to talk about them. There are no words for them. The theory of the unverbalised in human behaviour gives us a natural science way of explaining many things the Freudians now call 'unconscious complexes,' 'suppressed wishes' and the like. In other words we can now come back to natural science in our study of emotional behaviour. Our emotional life grows and develops like our other sets of habits. But do our emotional habits, once implanted, suffer from disuse ? Can they be put away and out-grown like our manual and verbal habits ?"[1]

The study of the behaviour of the individual as a whole, is, in the behaviourist view, based upon the contention that hands, larynx and viscera learn together and function together. That is to say that normal habits, habits of talking and thinking, and visceral habits are not only built up side by side but are all operative in any specific activity. "Under the influence of social demands the young developing human who has well entered into his world of speech has to put on his verbal and visceral habits simultaneously with his manual habits."[2] Of these three divisions of habit the verbal organization comes to be dominant and memory is then defined as the functioning of the 'verbal part of a total habit.' But Watson makes

---

[1]Behaviourism, page 130.
[2]Behaviourism, page 202.

a significant exception to this rule of *pari passu* formation of habits. All organizations put on in infancy, and all organizations put on throughout life where visceral segments preponderate are, he says, unaccompanied by the corresponding verbal habits. On this he bases the inability of children to 'remember' the activities of their early childhood and brings forward this view in opposition to the Freudian doctrine of repression of the pleasurable under social pressure.

'I believe the whole of Freud's "unconscious" can be adequately cared for along the lines I have indicated. The Freudians have no positive evidence to offer in contraversion; at least they have offered none.'[1]

The fact that the formation of visceral habits throughout life is not accompanied by correspondingly verbal habit formation is attributed by Watson to the lack of any demand from society of such verbal organization and indeed to the barrier opposed by convention to the discussion of such subjects.

The point of interest for us is as to how the behaviourist applies the doctrines we have outlined to the study of man's behaviour as a whole. 'Temperament' we have seen does not exist for him but 'personality' is allowed a place. Watson devotes a chapter to the discussion of personality. 'I define personality as the sum of activities that can be discovered by actual observation of behaviour over a long enough time to give reliable information.

---

[1]Behaviourism, page 210.

In other words personality is but the end product of our habit systems. Our procedure in studying personality is the making and plotting of a cross section of the activity stream. Among these activities, however, there are dominant systems in the manual field (occupational), in the language field (great talker, raconteur, silent thinker) and in the visceral field (afraid of people, shy, given to outbursts, loving to be petted, and in general what is called emotional). These dominant systems are obvious, easy to observe, and they serve as the basis for most of the rapid judgments we make about the personalities of individuals. It is upon the basis of the few dominant systems that we classify personalities.'[1]

The behaviourist further believes that the situation of the moment calls forth always in a predominating degree one or other of these three determining factors. The mark of what is commonly called integration is such a functioning of the three systems as to allow the one of which the dominance is required to function at its maximum efficiency. The difficulty of estimating an individual's 'emotional make up', that is his degree of visceral organization, is admitted, and these peculiarities which make for difficulty in relationship with others are looked upon as resulting from the persistence of unorganized infantile reactions carried over into adult life. Clearly on this basis the key to the growth of a 'healthy' personality and to the recovering of a 'sick' one lies in the vague word 'conditioning.'

---

[1]Behaviourism, page 220.

'You can, by conditioning, not only build up the behaviour complications, patterns and conflicts in diseased personalities but also by the same process lay the foundations for the onset of actual organic changes which result finally in infections and lesions '[1] and again

'There must be both unlearning the things we have already learned (and the unlearning may be an active unconditioning process or just disuse) and learning the new things which is always an active process.   Thus the only way thoroughly to change personality is to remake the individual by changing his environment in such a way that new habits have to form.   The more completely they change the more personality changes.   Few individuals can do this unaided.   That is why we go on year in and year out with the same old personality. Some day we shall have hospitals devoted to helping us to change our personality because we can change the personality as easily as we can change the shape of the nose only it takes more time.'[2]

Easy and attractive as this sounds there is yet a danger spot in the shape of the 'internal environment' which through verbal organization may be carried over into any given external surroundings.

The validity of the substitute which the behaviourist proposes for the 'unconscious' of Freudian theory, is not fortunately a subject which we are

---

[1]Behaviourism, page 246.
[2]Ibid, page 247.

called upon to discuss.   We are occupied with the question which touches us much more nearly.   This is no less than the question of whether the theory which we have outlined above is not a final blow to the purpose which we have in hand.   We have sought laboriously in the thought of many centuries for signs of a theory of 'temperament' which could help in modern requirements.

Are we at the end of the search not only to admit that it has failed, but to believe that the very act of prosecuting such an inquiry constitutes in itself an act of hostility to the progress of psychology in true scientific manner ?   Watson makes some severe strictures on those psychologists who have in time past put forward various theories on topics which they believed to be within their province. James's theory of emotion has, he claims, hung up the whole prospect of psychology for half a century. Theories of temperament would doubtless come under like condemnation.   Must we then discard .them altogether and agree that the long line of inquirers from Hippocrates to Jung have followed throughout a deceptive trail.

We may be loth to believe that all the classifications and theories of temperament which we have studied are entirely without foundation.   We may feel that convincing and attractive as Watson's exposition may be, it yet tends to over-simplification of the problem and that when his system is complete he also will feel the need to express differences in behaviour in terms which will convey a definite meaning to the man unlearned in anatomy and physiology.   But we must concede that the study of the behaviourist doctrine leaves with us the salutary conviction that we must be prepared, if in the light of further experiments it appears to be required of us, to abandon many of our cherished phrases and to substitute for them more mechanical elaborations of simple physiological processes.

CHAPTER XI

SUMMARY AND CONCLUSION

THE account which has been given in the previous pages of differing theories of temperament is not claimed as exhaustive. It is hoped, however, that the theories here expounded have at least served to emphasize some of the attitudes which have been, and are still, adopted towards this most controversial question. It was realized at the outset that the historical investigation that we proposed might end in one of three ways. It might have been that, after tracing the development of different theories we should be able to say 'Such and such a factor occurs in all the accounts of temperaments which we have considered; this then is obviously the essence of temperament and a definition can be framed accordingly.' We have not, it is clear, found any such universally admitted factor. Another possibility which had to be recognized was that at the end we might feel compelled to admit that not merely had no common factor emerged, but that we found no evidence in the accounts we had studied to justify the assumption that any such temperamental factor exists. To take this line would not necessarily imply that we had joined the ranks of the behaviourists but it would at least mean that we believed that individual differences in behaviour can be fully explained on certain well defined lines and that in consequence we do not feel the need of introducing such a concept as that of temperament. However optimistic we may be as to the future emergence of such an explanation we must admit that it is not yet ready. In the meantime, it may be at least a matter of convenience to postulate a temperamental determinant to denote certain differences in behaviour of which the true nature is still unknown. When we speak of knowing the true nature of such differences we do not mean merely the identification of the particular physiological functions or the inter-relations of functions which appear to produce a specific reaction. We include also the understanding of the process in virtue of which total reactions, which are themselves different, retain for a given individual in the presence of diverse stimuli, certain constant factors. Even Mr. J. B. Watson could not stricture us severely if we would agree that the use of the term is merely a matter of convenience and that we would be content to let it go in a more enlightened day. We would bind ourselves to resist the temptation to hypostatize a term, and we would refuse to impute to a term of convenience an active causality.

The third possibility which presented itself was that even though we should fail to find unanimity of agreement upon any one aspect we might yet feel entitled to abstract a little from one conception and a little from another and so put together a composite definition. We might then say 'That factor which is indicated by the characteristics we have described shall from this time be known as temperament and on it all further investigations shall be based.' Such a proceeding might be arbitrary but it might also be useful and it would gain the approval of those who believe that a preliminary hypothesis is indispensable to successful experiment. We may remember that Roback, for example, criticised the American experimentalists for their lack of theoretical background. It would perhaps be too much to assume that a cut and dried definition is to be taken as evidence of an adequate supporting theory, but if we adopt the necessary reservations it may be at least a harmless exercise to follow this course and seek to evolve a definition which is composite and conciliatory. The reservations we have already outlined; we are seeking a term of convenience which must yet be circumscribed to correspond with well defined observable phenomena.

At the risk of making a tedious repetition we must then pass rapidly in review the theories we have outlined and select from them the points which we require. It will be remembered that Richerand's exposition of the prototypes of the four classical temperaments gave support to the idea of demarcation in respect of variability in speed of reaction, and in maintenance of the original level of activity. A similar emphasis can be discerned in Ach's later classifications and an analogous conception is to be found in Watson's general activity level. We have also seen that McDougall postulates a general factor of 'temper' which manifests itself in respect of strength, persistence, and affectability in the sense of extent of influence by pleasure or pain. Ignoring for the moment the question raised by the introduction of 'affectability' we find again a similar emphasis on speed and duration. In the recent work of Ach, based on his investigations of willed action we found a classification based on 'feeling and willing capacity' in which the position of an individual in respect of 'temperament' was defined by the two considerations of level of initial activity and duration of maintenance of this level. Reviewing these theories, spread out in time over many years, and issuing from investigations of widely different natures we may perhaps be justified in hoping that the similarity of line of demarcation which, as analysed, they all present, may be something more than mere accident or than mere perversion of scientific deduction. But in the course of our survey, we were faced by the complications ensuing from the inclusion of emotional disturbance and this inclusion was seen to be inevitable. That some reactions characterised as emotional are innate was admitted even by the behaviourist school. The controversy as to how great this number may be is not immediately important to our discussion.

The question with which we are concerned is not so much whether most so called specific 'emotional reactions' are innate or conditioned but the general nature of the effect of any emotional reaction upon individual behaviour, and the variations in respect of this effect which may be

K

traced. General agreement was reached as to the close connexion which exists between emotional disturbance and bodily symptoms, but the constitution of an emotion was in wide dispute. This difficulty may be avoided by concentrating upon the recognized external signs of emotional disturbance, and these signs are to be sought, to some extent, in certain characteristic bodily experiences but more particularly in the degree of speeding up or retardation of the normal general activity level.

Modern research would appear to have established that 'emotional reactions' are intimately connected with the functioning of the endocrine glands. If the process of adjustment to environment is viewed from the physiological standpoint, the endocrine glands together with the vegetative nervous system are seen to co-operate with the central nervous system and to mediate response more particularly in respect of rapidity of initial activity and maintenance of its original level. A well established connexion has been worked out between the thyroid suprarenal system and the rapid adjustment to external stimuli. It is probable that further investigation will bring to light the co-operation or antagonism of other endocrine systems in this respect. The theory propounded by Watson is that if a stimulus calls forth an emotional reaction—while the external bodily manifestations may be inhibited—the glandular reaction remains, with the result that the existing activity is either reinforced or inhibited. This conflict between the two possible forces of reinforcement or inhibition is clearly a root difficulty. Its solution may be found in the nature of early 'conditioning' or it may prove to lie in the degree of co-operation of the endocrine systems. At the moment this can only be a matter of conjecture, but future investigation should elucidate it. Again it may prove that in endocrine relationships lies the clue to the explanation of the 'central emotional core' which has been suggested to some writers by scientific observation of certain peculiarities of behaviour. What would appear to emerge for our comfort is that this question of susceptibility to emotion which was shrouded in mystery and difficulty may prove to resolve itself into simplified components and that if such susceptibility is measured it will be by the estimation of such components, through these same factors of initial level and duration of maintenance with which the theories we have outlined have already made us familiar.

With the contribution of Ach the question of temperament was lifted on to the plane of volition and strength of determining tendencies. But his classification was based on activity level in respect of initial strength and duration of maintenance. When he talks of differences in 'feeling and willing capacity' and of 'innate determining tendencies' we have no reason to suppose that his investigations would suffer if these 'capacities' were ultimately analysed in terms of endocrine relationships and the 'conditionings' of environmental influences throughout life. That analysis is not yet ready and pending its production we may take the classification Ach has given, and without stressing its ultimate basis find in its co-ordinates a reinforcement of the theory of 'temperament' which is gradually emerging.

The 'types' of Jung are less amenable. It may perhaps be permitted to find in his functions of 'sensation,' 'thinking,' 'feeling' and intuition the marks of those factors of strength and continuity which we are anxious to stress, but it is clear that it is on the question of direction that the emphasis is chiefly laid. At this point it may be profitable to set down again the various factors in terms of which a classification has so far been attempted. If we use as bases the factors sensitivity, duration, direction, emotion, inhibition we can perhaps claim that we have in terms of modern psychology allowed for all groupings of which we have taken cognisance in our review. Using for convenience the old terms sanguine, choleric, phlegmatic and melancholic with the 'cautious' contributed by Ach, the resulting classification would be somewhat as follows:

Sanguine   high sensitivity, low persistence,
  Temperament outward direction, weak emotion-
               ality and little inhibition.

Choleric   high sensitivity, low persistence,
  Temperament both outward and inward direction,
               strong emotionality with little
               inhibition.

Phlegmatic   low sensitivity, high persistence,
  Temperament little outward or inward direction,
               weak emotionality with consider-
               able inhibition.

Melancholic Temperament	low sensitivity, low persistence, inward direction, strong emotionality but great inhibition.
Cautious Temperament	high sensitivity, high persistence, both inward and outward direction, moderate emotionality and inhibition. (In respect of emotionality and direction the judgment on the cautious temperament must be purely speculative.)

Such a classification would mean that the position of a given individual could only be indicated by a five dimensional graph. Convenience has doubtless given us a preference for the two dimensional and if we were allowed to manipulate experimentally the above classifications we might produce one of the following nature—

	Initial Speed.	Duration.
Sanguine	.. High ..	.. Low
Cautious	.. High ..	.. High
Phlegmatic	.. Low ..	.. High
Melancholic	.. Low ..	.. Low

Now if in respect of these four temperaments we compare with the broader classifications given above, we might call attention to the fact that a marked outward direction is connected with an initial high speed of reaction and a marked inward direction with a low initial speed. Similarly we might suggest that high duration implies certainly a moderate, and probably a low degree of emotionality and that conversely high emotionality would

appear to be incompatible with long duration.
We might perhaps be more accurate in suggesting
that high duration is connected essentially with a
distributed emotionality, low duration with an
undistributed affect. This recalls the '*tempérament
d'épargne*' and the '*tempérament de dépense*' of Fouillée.
This attempted combination is purely fanciful,
and so derived it can have no claim to exact consideration. We need therefore make no excuse for
having omitted the choleric temperament from
the table since its position was not clear. But
the point which would appear to raise an insistent
claim is that if ever an ultimate classification is
arrived at, based as it must surely be on spontaneous
manifestations in behaviour it must turn primarily
upon the questions of speed and time. Further
we may remind ourselves that such knowledge of
the working of the endocrine glands as we possess,
does in truth point to the fact that it is in respect of
these factors that their intermediacy in that process
of adjustment which we call behaviour makes
itself felt. It is along these lines that the evidence
of centuries of speculation upon the temperamental
problem has pointed. Even the question of
'direction'—the most difficult to bring into line—
may prove to reduce itself to the question of rapidity
and ease of reaction, determined by glandular
co-operation.

To speak of direction of effort is to suggest a
purposeful control. Rapidity and duration are
comparatively neutral terms, but direction calls
up at once a teleological conception. We are
then forced back to the controversy which in this

final review we have so far avoided, which centres round the purposive rôle of the emotions. It is clear that this is in turn only part of the wider difficulty of translating from the physiological to the psychological. The gulf between the two is often bridged by the adoption of a concept of 'psychic energy.' We have seen for example that McDougall speaks of emotion as 'indicative of an energy which works teleologically and which is therefore radically different from the energies of physical science.' If once this conception of two forms of energy—physical and psychic—were adopted many of the recalcitrant factors we have encountered would find a facile reconciliation. We might, for example, look upon the sentiments as supplying the psychic energy of the determining tendencies postulated by Ach. We have only to assume that the correspondence in properties between the two forms of energy is complete and the questions of quantity, continuity and direction assume also a comprehensible meaning. As to whether this assumption is justified must remain for the present a matter of opinion. On the one hand there is the pertinent criticism of the physicist which crystallises itself in the question 'What then is the unit of measurement in respect of psychic energy?' 'Ergs we know but by what scale do you propose to measure the capacity for work which, on your claim, should be the mark of psychic energy?' To this criticism it is sometimes replied that although the unit of measurement is not yet forthcoming and although therefore, in this respect the analogy between physcial and psychic energy must be admitted to be incomplete, yet the assumption of the hypothesis of psychic energy is justified because it has been found to be profitable as a starting point for further elaboration. It will then be interesting to see in what way, if we permitted this assumption, our own problem would be simplified. We must ignore the question of the means whereby the physical energy which results from metabolic processes is made available in the psychic sphere. There remains the question of the expenditure of the energy produced. It is assumed by those who talk about psychic energy that it has a seat and is capable of flux and of change of direction. If it is compared as is often the case, to the flowing of a stream then the important factors are its volume and the rate and direction of its flow; and these we must consider in reference to the different theories of temperament which we have put forward.

Evidence of the amount of energy available and of the direction which it tends to take spontaneously, together with its speed of working, is sought for chiefly in the method of attack in conative processes.

Emotion is regarded generally as an aspect of psychic energy, but the question of emotion is attacked from two different points of view. On the one hand there is what is referred to as 'the general affective tone'—the 'tonus' expressed, for example by Dr. Berman in terms of intravisceral pressure.

In reference to the 'stream of energy' this would appear to depend upon the general level of the stream, that is upon the quantity and continuity of output. Such a general level has a direct result upon effort put forward in action. It will probably account for, or at least move parallel with, the factors of volitional perseveration and speed emphasized in the Downey Will Temperament Test.

The other aspect of emotion is its connexion with the working of specific instincts. Whether it is regarded simply as the 'feeling aspect of an instinct' or more particularly as the 'conscious aspect of a curtailed instinct,' it is bound up with the degree of successful expression of instinctive tendencies.

It is necessary to connect this view of specific emotion with the concept of psychic energy. The obvious use of emotion is here to effect a relaxation of tension by the discharge of energy. Such energy if undischarged, would constitute a 'load' and would interfere with successful inhibition. Continuing the stream metaphor, emotion is here connected with the clearance of the path of the flowing energy.

According as one or other aspect of emotion is emphasized it appears that either general emotional tone has an immediate bearing on conation or that any attempted conation carries with it the possibility of a specific emotion.

The questions of the production and consumption of energy do not exhaust the possibilities of its consideration. There remains the question of the transformation of energy, and on the possibilities of this transformation educational effort bases its justification. That form of energy transformation which goes by the name of sublimation is familiar in connexion with the contributions of the psycho-analysts to the investigation of personality.

In addition to the question of amount, speed, and continuity of average flow is the further question of increased production demanded by an emergency situation. This idea of emergency production corresponds with the conception of a reserve supply of energy and with the idea that the organism is not normally working at full strength. It is claimed that in the case of specific instincts, additional energy is available at need to meet the demands of an exceptional situation.

The line of thought suggested by emergency resources calls up the conception of integration familiar in modern psychological writings. It has been noted that Fouillée connected integration with the '*tempérament d'apargne*', disintegration with the '*tempérament de dèpense.*' This is not necessarily to exalt the niggardly as opposed to the lavish expenditure of energy, but to recommend that economy of energy which gives to each situation the measure it requires, which is the unmistakable sign of a successful integration of resources.

Again the idea of integration suggests at once the idea of will. According to one view, a willed act is precisely that act which shows greatest evidence of integration, accomplished through the working out of the instinct of self-assertion. So the concept of integration as the marshalling and controlling of energy could easily be brought into line with the concept of a 'Will-Temperament.'

It has however, been pointed out that it is not clear whether in the researches of Miss Downey, this is the precise significance attached to the 'will.'

It would appear then, that most of the conflicting terms met with in the study of the literature available on the subject of temperament, may if we wish be reconciled in terms of the concept of psychic energy. In it may be comprehended the questions—In what direction, at what rate, with what power of control, or with what possibilities of reserve is the individual moving? How lavishly or with what economy does he direct his reactions? To what extent are these reactions knit together? How smoothly or with what irregularities does his course persist? To what extent in future, given like conditions, can his course be predicted? Such are the questions on which the discussions on temperament, personality, or types here considered have turned. The question would still arise 'Where in all this is temperament to be found and how is its definition to be evolved?' A distinction was made in the introduction between 'disposition,' 'temper' and 'temperament' in the sense defined by Dr. McDougall. 'Disposition' was held to denote the sum total of the instincts and their relative strength in any individual. It is admitted that an assessment of the 'disposition' of the subject is an indispensable part of any attempt to estimate his 'personality.' Confusion arises when an attempt is made to combine in this division the estimate of 'temperament' with that of 'disposition' and even of 'character.'

Viewed from the standpoint of energy, the disposition would seem to be waiting an agreement as to the relative amount of energy available to specific instincts. So far the instincts of sex, and of self-assertion compete in contemporary writings for the first place in strength and consequently in psychic energy. So far as the estimate of the individual is concerned, however, all that is possible is to arrange a list of the recognised instincts in order of probable strength, based on results obtained from observation of reactions, or from a questionnaire. It would seem to be a great simplification if the 'disposition,' regarded in this sense, could be considered as a distinct and separate factor in the estimate of personality.

'Temper' was defined as the expression of the way in which the conative impulses work. This refers to the working of each separate instinct and corresponds to Shand's idea of the function of temperament. If the criterion of energy is applied to this conception of Temper, it is clear that it is primarily in connexion with the direction taken by the conative impulses that the correspondence would hold good. The question of continuity of effort would also be involved. There is thus an obvious connexion between 'Temper' and the Psychological Types outlined by Jung.

'Temperament' itself was provisionally defined as the sum of the effects upon the mental life of the metabolic changes that are constantly going on in all the tissues of the body. With this conception the quantitative aspects of energy will comply easily, so also will considerations of speed and continuity of flow. The question of direction taken by the energy produced will not however be included and while it may embrace the idea of general affective tone it will have no part in the conception of specific emotions.

Taking these definitions it would again appear that what emerges as required is a Temper-Temperament combination. Such a concept would embrace certain well-defined features of the individual personality, the knowledge of which would form a valuable key to his educational treatment.

On the temper-temperament basis could rest Jung's 'Types' and Berman's 'Endocrine Personalities' and any attempt to classify on the slow or quick reaction basis. From this angle the problem of integration could be attacked, working on the disposition through the temperament.

Turning to the Downey Will-Temperament test the agreement does not appear to be so complete. The trait of aggressiveness, for example, emphasized in these tests belongs clearly to the sphere of 'disposition' rather than of 'temperament,' the question of 'perseveration' is more amenable but presents difficulties according to the angle from which it is attacked. 'Freedom from load' might easily be brought into line, but 'susceptibility to suggestion' again belongs rather to the 'disposition.'

On the whole, it would seem advisable, not to combine the Will and the Temperament in one connotation but to attempt a formulation of the temperament which would include those aspects discussed above under the terms 'Temper and Temperament.' Such a formulation would cover, the direction, continuity, speed of flow, and reserve power of the psychic energy available in the individual and would determine the extent to which this is a general factor covering all activities or a specific factor colouring the work of individual instincts.

But on the whole we must conclude that however valuable the concept of psychic energy may prove to be in the building up for example of the technique of psycho-analysis, yet the mere postulation of its existence does not in itself advance materially the search for a temperamental factor. If there is any validity in the conclusions we have been able to draw without invoking the aid of a psychic energy concept then it would appear sufficient to assume that further efforts should be conducted on the lines of investigating differences in speed of reaction and in duration of maintenance of the initial level of activity. It may be advisable to drop the term 'temperament' altogether and so hope to escape from the welter of controversies in which it is entangled. If the claim of speed and continuity is substantiated then perhaps 'tempo' would be considered a not unsuitable term to denote this factor, but the name is comparatively unimportant. We may perhaps frame a tentative definition. The 'tempo' of an individual should be considered as the factor which influences his reactions to non-specialised situations in respect of speed of initial response and duration of activity level. The word 'non-specialised' is included as a preliminary safeguard against an obvious criticism which must be met when we come to consider the nature of those situations which present themselves as suitable for experimental investigation of the 'tempo' of any given individual. But before proceeding to this difficult question it may be wise to add to this tentative definition a few qualifying remarks. It is probable that the 'tempo' of an individual is a direct function of the inter-action of endocrine systems which in turn is dependent upon general bodily structure. It may be that in time the exact connexion between structure, endocrine functioning, and reaction may be laid bare. A resulting classification in terms of structure, or predominance of specific glandular functionings may then be evolved. It will yet remain true that for the understanding of its effect upon behaviour we shall require an expression of these effects in terms of some such factors as we have indicated.

There are many questions which present themselves: 'Why this zeal for classification ?' 'Why this attempt to disintegrate behaviour ?' 'Will not all such differentiations tend to disappear when the endocrine determinants can be regulated by injection ?' To the first two it is only possible to reply by pointing to the train of argument which we have followed. An eagerness to classify must be taken as evidence of a desire to understand ; the classification can never be final or complete but its value is the attempt which it embodies to determine lines of demarcation. These lines appear to disintegrate the unity of behaviour but this is not a necessary corollary, and in any case it must be admitted that a unity which is procured at the cost of inadequate understanding cannot in itself be a desideratum.

The third question as to the regulation of temperament raises many points. We have seen the idea of the 'mixture' in the writing of Hippocrates and it has retained its appeal to the minds of men. It embodies the doctrine of harmony in which philosophers of all ages have sought to reconcile conflicting distortions. It is bound up with the quantitative aspect of consideration which is now so familiar in psychological work. But between the idea of a desirable mixture and the conceptions of disposition and temperament which have been considered there is a certain antithesis.

On the one hand is the idea of an inherited measure of more or less of this or that instinct, of physical or psychic energy. Over against this is the idea of a well balanced mixture. So soon, however, as a practical proposal for establishing the 'mixture' is brought forward it arouses a general feeling of repugnance. The idea of tampering with the natural endowment is looked upon as either ludicrous or sacrilegious. There is for example Bernard Shaw's indictment in his preface to St. Joan—'As to the new rites which would be the saner Joan? The one to whom the concentrated wafer was the very body of the virtue that was her salvation, or the one who looked forward to a precise and convenient regulation of her health and her desires by a nicely calculated diet of thyroid extract, adrenalin, pituitrin and insulin with pick-me-up of hormone stimulant. Which is the healthier mind, the saintly mind or the monkey gland mind?'

So little is known at present about the possibilities of regulating the secretions of the endocrine glands that it cannot be profitable to discuss the ultimate effects upon behaviour which such manipulations will produce. It is probable that in the light of greater knowledge it will arouse no more hostility than any other form of surgical and medicinal treatment. There can be nothing inherently sacrosanct in the tendency of an individual to react in a given way and no greater intrinsic objection to interference by injection of thyroid extract than to removal of adenoids or administration of insulin.

CHAPTER XII

SOME TENTATIVE SUGGESTIONS

WE have now finished the analysis on which we embarked and have drawn from it the conclusions expressed in the last chapter, and there is a strong temptation to abandon any further effort. We may take up a neutral position and say :—

'The study of the different theories which we have completed would appear to indicate that if there is in human behaviour an irreducible factor which may be known as temperament or 'tempo' its manifestations must be looked for along the lines of rapidity of natural response and in duration of the disturbances produced. That is to say it is essentially a time factor.'

With this pronouncement we might safely leave the further issue in other hands. Such an attitude might be condemned as unenterprising but it would doubtless be the most discreet. The next stage of inquiry is of necessity a difficult one. It would consist in the attempt to bring this factor under the conditions of a controlled experiment.

If we have any hope that it may be accepted on the basis of quantitative analysis in which at the moment the hope of psychology is centred we must manufacture situations and units in which its effect can be measured. The difficulty of the task is widely recognised. In the report of the Consultative Committee of the Board of Education on Psychological Tests of Educable Capacity, Temperament and Character are bracketed together and the conclusion reached is that so far no method of estimating either has been found which can be considered more reliable than that of careful observation.

'Few however would as yet pretend that such tests can merit anything more than an experimental interest ; and in their present state the methods are unsuited for practical employment in this country.

'In assessing temperament and character, therefore, we are bound to fall back upon the method of observation in place of the method of experiment.'[1]

But the time must surely come when we are no longer bound to fall back upon observation but may hope to make of temperament an experimental study in conditions which approximate to those of the laboratory. It may be argued that many attempts at experimental investigation have already been made and that valuable results have been obtained. To this we must reply that while undoubtedly much valuable information has been acquired, yet the experiments in question did not measure and did not claim to measure any such irreducible constituent of behaviour as that which we have suggested, of which the existence is awaiting demonstration or disproof. The difficulties which have to be met in the type of investigation would

---

[1] Page 59.

appear to be of a two-fold nature. There has been in the first place an uncertainty as to the nature of the object of measurement. And in the second an inability to devise situations in which this factor should find a direct unqualified expression.

One of the criticisms which Dr. Roback brings against the Downey Will Temperament tests is that the conditions under which they were executed do not approximate to 'life situations.' It will be remembered that the medium of the test was the execution of handwriting under certain conditions so that the factors which they claimed to measure were speed—aggressiveness—persistence. These were considered in reference to freedom from load, resistance to opposition and finality of judgment. The whole reaction was taken as a measurement of psychic momentum.

Without returning again to the confusion which surrounds these factors, we may try to consider dispassionately the merits of such a testing medium. The first criticism which would suggest itself would be that the situation chosen is not in correspondence with the object of the investigation. We are accustomed to consider vaguely that handwriting is an index of character, but we connect it too closely with acquired habits to admit it as a satisfactory measure of spontaneous activity. Again it might be argued that the mere imposition of instructions constitutes a 'determining tendency' which may inhibit the unfettered expression of the temperamental factor. However carefully the conditions of the experiment were designed with a view to eliminating the irrelevant considerations we are

left with a feeling after a more natural setting—
after what Dr. Roback calls a 'life situation.' It
may be argued on the other hand that if the factor
which we are investigating is really a fundament of
behaviour, then its presence must be felt in all
reactions however much they may be conditioned.
We should readily agree that this is so but would
point to the difficulty of disintegrating this particular factor from the many other components
which combine to produce the observed resultant
behaviour. It is the elimination of irrelevant
factors from the setting of the experiment which
constitutes the peculiar difficulty of the task.

This difficulty is not of course confined to experiments on temperament but it is complicated in
this connexion by the requirement that the conditions required must be a 'life situation.' As to
what exactly is the implication of the phrase 'life
situation' it will then be necessary to inquire.
Since it is in itself a rather vague and non-technical
term we are not compelled to convert it into the
exact language of experimental technique. We may
perhaps take it to mean that it implies a situation
which is not apparently controlled by explicit
instructions issued by the experimenter. The
nature of an experiment involves both an experimenter and a definite line of pursuit; this is at
least the case if the object of the experiment has
been specifically defined. If this object should happen to be then, the investigation of temperament, it
would appear to follow, that if this requirement of a
'life situation' is a sound one the subject of the
experiment must be unaware not only of the object

of the experiment (this is a common requirement in many psychological experiments) but also, that the situation itself is under the influence of specific external control. This condition should not in itself present an insuperable difficulty.

There are two methods by which the question of selection of the conditions of a controlled experiment on temperament might be approached. The one would be to consider some of the uncontrolled situations of life in which 'temperament' is generally held to exert its influences. It would then be necessary to analyse these situations and the response which was described as 'temperamental' with a view to ascertaining whether the circumscribed temperament which we have outlined could here be isolated. Such an analysis should also, if successful, bring to light those aspects of the situation which were the essence of the stimulus. The other method of attack would be from an entirely different angle. It would consist in the postulate of an isolated 'temperament' and the experiment would take the form of eliciting, by a process of trial and error the nature and magnitude of the stimulus which would rouse this 'temperament' to reaction.

Either of these lines of inquiry would be a fascinating one. Since if we follow the second we are less likely to be side-tracked on to more complicated paths, it may be well to begin by a brief attempt to ascertain the activities of an isolated temperament.

Physiologically we should postulate of course the endocrine glands and their connexions with the nervous system. We should wish to eliminate as far as possible all engran traces of previous experience, all 'complexes' and all acquired 'mental sets.' We should further postulate that this 'temperament' was quiescent and this we might describe as its position of equilibrium. A stimulus is now applied with intent to produce a disturbance. According to the reasoning of mechanics one of three things may happen.

The 'temperament' may after a varying length of time return to its initial position, it may on the other hand, recede further and further from this position, or in the third case it may take up immediately a new position as the result of the disturbance. According to the category of its reaction it would be designated as of stable, unstable or neutral equilibrium. We cannot press the mathematical analogy too far but there is perhaps one other helpful suggestion which can be derived from it. It may be that the stimulus we apply produces no disturbance either in virtue of its quality or of its intensity. That is to say it is our task to find the minimum stimulus which will produce a definite temperamental response. We might say that we are seeking the limen of disturbance. Looked at from the psychological aspect we may say that the effect of any disturbance is to distract attention. The distraction of attention may not in itself, it will be argued, be accompanied by any such inner disturbance as goes by the name of emotion. Thus, in the consideration of our dis-embodied temperament, it may be supposed that a gradual increase in the intensity of the light of the room in which it is placed, would not involve any temperamental disturbance although the stimulus so provided would evoke a slight re-adjustant response on the part of the organism as a whole. If on the other hand the electric light was suddenly switched on and immediately switched off again there would be a 'distraction of attention but we should expect that the isolated temperament would return very quickly to its initial position of equilibrium. In the event, however, of a marked deviation being effected by so comparatively slight a stimulus, we should look for still greater deviation in response to a stimulus of greater intensity and we should be inclined to characterize the tempera-ment as markedly unstable.

We might proceed in our imaginary experiments with a series of stimuli acting on different sense organs and discover whether the 'temperament' in question showed particular irritability in respect of any one such stimulus. We might try com-binations of stimuli and mark the resultant disturb-ance. Many questions would arise which would call for investigation. Perhaps the most urgent would be as to whether on the part of the 'isolated temperament' there could be any response to a stimulus which had not acquired significance through previous experience. By the result of that experiment the very claim of temperament to a separate existence would stand or fall. We know however that we cannot isolate temperament and put it on a laboratory table for experimental investigation ; but before leaving this line of thought we may perhaps with profit carry it one

stage further. Let us imagine once again that an
'isolated temperament' were actually placed on a
table and that its position was indicated by two
rectangular co-ordinates. Now suppose that a
stimulus in the form of a series of intermittent
noises were applied ; and that in response, while
the noise continued, the temperament changed its
position on the table. Such movement might
oscillate but at the time when the stimulus was
finally discontinued there would be a measurable
deviation from the original position of equilibrium.

A second experiment might then be undertaken
in respect of observation of the time taken to return
to the initial position of equilibrium. The measurement of time would seem to be the one aspect
which can be carried over into the region of practical experiment. By what means however are we
to estimate equilibrium positions and divergence
from them. This would seem to be an insoluble
difficulty unless it too can be reduced to a time basis.
There are various measurements which may be
postulated. We can, in theory at least, measure the
time between the application of the stimulus and
the first noticeable response to it. We could in
theory measure the whole time taken up by the
response, and again as we have already suggested
we may measure the time taken to return to the
old position. It might be that the analyses of
these respective time measurements might lead to
the formulation of a mathematical connection between them, that for example the ratio of the total
time taken up by the response to the time of duration of the stimulus might be held for the purpose

of the experiment to denote the measure of divergence from the initial position of equilibrium, or again that for a given individual the mathematical connexion if any could be shown to exist, between the time taken before the beginning of the response and the time taken between cessation of the stimulus and the final return may be held to measure the degree of stability. Translated into practice this could only be interpreted as a measure of time in respect of retardation of a given task and of the time taken to return to this occupation after the cessation of the stimulus.

Such change in speed, has further, as we have already suggested to be accomplished without the suspected influence of external deliberate interference and in the absence of any great significance in the nature of the stimulus or in the previous reaction which it is designed to disturb. In saying that the stimulus should not be of great significance we mean that it should not call into activity any organised 'engram complex' which has resulted from previous experience. That such conditions are difficult to secure it will readily be admitted, but it should be possible, after a necessarily prolonged period of trial and error to arrive eventually at an experimental setting which is in at least approximate correspondence with laboratory requirements.

We may now turn from the hypothesis of an isolated temperament to the consideration of some situations in ordinary life in which the influence of 'temperament' is commonly thought to be identified. It would probably be admitted by most people that such situations may be reduced to those in which a disturbance makes itself felt in a familiar environment. We might also claim that the disturbance would itself be qualified as of no great significance. The reactions of an individual to such disturbances as the loss of a fortune, of employment, or of a well-loved friend, would not be chosen as examples of temperamental bias. In these cases the stimulus would be recognised as of real significance, and the reaction as invoking the activity of the acquired sentiments of a lifetime. The influence of temperament would doubtless make itself felt even in reactions of such a nature but its share would be difficult to isolate. It is rather in those incidents where the disturbance would appear to be disproportionate to the significance of its cause that the evidence of the work of temperament would be considered most observable. This view would accord well with the hypothesis of an indefinitely small stimulus, and the limen of irritability which we discovered above.

It is perhaps possible to circumscribe the situation a little more without over-stepping the limits of common agreement. A man's reactions to enforced though mild discomfort, to acceptance of a temporarily changed environment, and to the exigencies of love are generally believed to be indicative of temperamental bias. It is not, for example without significance that the conditions of travelling are held to constitute a test of friendship, or that the incompatibility of temperament which results in a broken engagement is held to show itself most consistently in incidents which are themselves trivial. But for the purposes of controlled experiment even the most trivial of such instances is far too complicated, and such a factor as inhibition through ideals of conduct must assert an appreciable influence on the observable reaction. The experimenter cannot moreover organize a train journey across Europe for his subjects, nor has he the means of observing in all its aspects the behaviour of people to one another. We might imagine ourselves to be the spectators of reactions of individual travellers to an enforced wait at a frontier station. It would be necessary to postulate that the individuals so observed were comfortable and well fed, that they were in no danger of losing a train, and had no secret urgent worries—that the required reaction was in short simply one of waiting. If individual A paces restlessly up and down, then sits down, only to get up again and so oscillates unevenly between the only two reactions possible to him, while B on the other hand sits calmly smoking a pipe throughout the wait, the observer might with perhaps some degree of justice infer that their respective reactions were indicative of a temperamental difference. This inference would be strengthened if on resuming the journey A carried over the marks of disturbance while B showed an equally rapid response to the now changed conditions.

We might again become the imaginary spectators of a scene in which two people have to choose at which out of three restaurants they shall dine. We should need to postulate that there was not to either of them any determining cause of preference in respect of any of the three possibilities and that the dinner was not in itself regarded as a function of importance. We notice however, that to the suggestion of A that restaurant X will do quite well, B replies that perhaps Y might be better and that on A's agreeing that Y will do, B brings forward the claims of Z, not in the least because he is animated by a 'spirit of perversity' but because, faced by a choice, in the absence of any determining factor, his speed of reaction is slower than that of A. Such oscillation on the part of B could not in any case be taken as evidence of vacillation in the face of momentous decision. The two incidents which we have selected at random are offered only as a rough approximation to a situation in which the 'time factor' in adjustment approaches an uncomplicated expression. It may be argued that the incidents chosen are in their triviality unsuited for a dignified discussion of a scientific subject. To this we may reply that nothing can be more trivial and at the same time more scientific than the representation of the earth by a dot and of the sun by a small circle. The real criticism to which the incidents selected lay themselves open is not on the score of triviality but of complication. It would be easy to supply a long list of such examples. Variations in ease of adaptability to a holiday environment, or to an atmosphere of work on return, to the exigencies of an examination room, are all instances in which other things being equal, the temperamental factor may be thought to exercise a determining influence. But it is the difficulty of making other things equal, that is, the elimination of irrelevant factors, which makes such instances though trivial too complicated for consideration from the experimental point of view.

In the lives of children we may hope to find a somewhat simplified situation and greater possibility of control. We hear a child called 'dreamy', and this does not necessarily mean that he is engaged all the time with a rich inner life of phantasy. It refers rather to the delay which occurs in switching off from one activity to another, and which results in an apparently inexplicable slowness. The process of dressing and the preparation for the daily walk bring out a difference in speed of reaction in individual children which appears to be indicative of a corresponding temperamental difference. But even in these comparatively simple conditions we cannot be sure that other factors are eliminated. It would only be in the repeated manifestation of retarded beginnings in differing situations that even the foreshadowing of evidence could be claimed. At the opposite end of the scale is the child who is alluded to as 'excitable.' He is not necessarily bad tempered or unduly demonstrative of affection, he is just 'excitable,' that is to say he appears to show a disproportionate activity in reference to a stimulus which may in itself be slight. The outlet of this activity is apt to differ and from the point of view of measurement is not amenable to scientific investigation. Already, children who are designated over-excitable are suspected of hyper-activity in respect of the rate of functioning of the thyroid glands. Here may be sought the physiological cause of the conditions but its effects in behaviour are to be looked for in great rapidity of response and prolonged continuance of the disturbance created.

Is there any means of testing these vaguely characterized differences by controlled experiment? We should expect that if it can be done anywhere the school would offer the best opportunity for a standardized situation. In school, children live in an environment which is at least comparatively uniform but it may be objected that the school environment is essentially a specialized one and moreover one controlled largely by specific instructions. At the beginning of this chapter we recorded the conclusion that one essential feature of experiments on temperament is that the subject must be unaware of controlling instructions. Only with this safeguard can the influence of inhibitions set up by determining tendencies be measured. It may be asked 'In what way does the child's temperament in the sense in which we have defined it, make itself felt in his school day?' We are familiar with the differing degrees of ease with which children will turn from one lesson to another. But to diagnose this as the result of temperament would be to ignore such relevant factors as variation in particular interests. If however the same lag should occur between all consecutive lessons and if the hypothesis of physical unfitness had been eliminated we might perhaps regard it as indicative of a fundamental difference. The function of perseveration, in the narrower sense of delay in cessation of the stimulus (even after the actual stimulus has been discontinued) would be relevant, but this would not constitute a difficulty since it would appear to be closely connected with the temperamental outfit as we have defined it.

We may take an imaginary case of a class of children of seven years of age, listening with interest to a story of which the climax has not yet been reached. We may stipulate for the absence of any signs of lethargy or of restlessness. The condition of the children might be described as one of equilibrium. They are reacting to the present situation in the way required of it. We may imagine that suddenly a cat jumps in at the window. The stimulus possesses a slight emotional significance but arouses no fear. The probable reaction will be one of laughter. The cat is quietly taken out and the teacher returns to the story. Individual children will show variations in the speed with which they will return to their former state of equilibrium controlled entirely by interest in the lesson. This will be shown by such external signs as spasmodic laughter and general restlessness. There will be in the majority of cases an oscillation between the stimulus of the cat and that of the story and the resultant reaction will approach gradually to the initial equilibrium position.

A similar oscillation will occur for example, after a fire drill. The ringing of the fire bell may be described as a stimulus of a slightly emotional character—this is so even when the children know that the practice is to take place. With older children the introduction of visitors into a class room will call out similar differences in time reaction.

In the examples we have taken the stimulus has been of no great significance, and the reactions we have described have been supposed to be spontaneous. What is required in each case has been a return to the initial equilibrium position and, in the absence of controlling inhibitions, the time taken to secure this return will vary.

Another type of situation might be imagined—that in which the required reaction is not a return to original conditions but the adaptation to new ones. This was the type already alluded to in connection with the change over of lessons, and in an earlier part of the chapter in the example of adaptation to holiday conditions or to a return to work. Working along these lines it might be possible in time to work out standardised situations in school life which may have a definite objective value. The danger of precise instructions may perhaps be eliminated or at least reduced by the factor of choice. We could imagine, for example, children confronted with a choice of three tasks of no great difficulty but of equal interest with which without reference to a time limit they are free to occupy themselves. This situation is analagous to that of the choice of restaurant discussed before. What would appear to suggest itself as of practical value would be a combination of these three types of experiment—one in which the time taken to return to a previous position of equilibrium is required, a second in which the time taken to take up another defined position is measured, and a third in which the delay resulting from unhampered choice is considered as the relevant abstraction. The details of the experiments which would meet these requirements have yet to be thought out and must necessarily be preceded by a long process

M

of trial and error and gradual elimination. Should they ever materialize and should the results so obtained show a reasonably high degree of correlation, we might then perhaps not unjustly claim that it would constitute some slight evidence of the existence of 'temperament' as an irreducible constituent of behaviour.

A short time ago there appeared in the newspapers a paragraph to the effect that the temperament of a very famous singer had been insured for the sum of over £6,000. It would be interesting to know what exactly the producer had in mind when he took this precaution. Presumably he was afraid that at the last moment the artist might fail to make an appearance, or that in the middle of the performance he might refuse to go on. The situation of a concert-hall is a specific one, the response required from an artist is equally specific. An artist who has contracted to make an appearance has presumably set up his 'determining tendencies' which will secure that the contract is fulfilled. If he fails to come it would appear from the angle of our discussion to imply that in respect of some new situation—internal or external—whether of small or great significance—he might manifest such rapidity of reaction and such deviation from the initial equilibrium position that a return to it within the time available is ruled out. The time factor is all important for the artist, the producer and the insurance agency, but it is doubtful whether they could be brought to admit that such a grandiose conception as that of temperament could in effect be reduced to such comparatively meagre proportions.

APPENDIX

'THE RÔLE OF TEMPERAMENT IN EDUCATIONAL THEORY AND PRACTICE '

THE study of the historical development of the theory of temperament which has formed the content of this book owed its original inception to a growing interest on the part of the author in the rôle of 'temperament' in the class room of the school. All those who have taught children of varying ages, in any type of school have become aware at an early stage in their career of difficulties in contact which they were wont to attribute to a vague, undefined, perhaps indefinable factor known as 'temperament.' On the one hand the young teacher has to weigh himself against the composite organism which is his class. From such a balance of personalities arises the familiar three-fold classification which confirms at one extreme the so called 'born teachers,' at the other those condemned as temperamentally unfitted for the particular variety of human contact which teaching demands, and between these two opposites the vast majority who contrive to preserve a reasonable degree of harmony between themselves and the class.

But much more important are the considerations which emerge when the teacher tries, as he must, to understand the individual members who make up the class. In every class of children there are some who would appear particularly to demand this study of their individual make-up ; in reality there is no child in whose case such a study will fail to be illuminating. The educational doctrines of to-day centre largely round the question of individual differences. To say this is to utter a truism. But when we analyse these differences as they are described in educational writings we find that emphasis is laid chiefly on differences in general intelligence, in specific abilities, and in relative strength of instinctive tendencies. The references to a temperamental factor in whatever sense it may be defined are vague and diffuse, although there are signs that the importance of such a factor is at least partially recognized. The modern conception of instinct has proved capable of supporting a whole system of educational theory. It has furnished a solution to many problems and the child's 'disposition,' in the sense defined by McDougall, has become the key to his educational treatment. Educational theorists have welcomed the term 'instinct' as a tool amenable to their purpose. But in the 'temperament' they are confronted with a much more uncompromising factor. Because it has been regarded as an incalculable factor it might from one point of view be regarded as definitely hostile to the purpose of education. But if the temperament is essentially a differentiating agent, it should prove a key to much which is unique in the child's individuality. It is precisely this individuality which is emphasized most strongly in any modern statement of the educational ideal and it would seem therefore that in the analysis of any such statement the temperament must be allowed a place.

We have drawn attention to the belief, widely held, that it is particularly in the relations of people, one to another that temperament is apt to exert its influence. The school is regarded as an agent for securing a profitable relationship between the child and his environment. Of this environment it is probable that his fellow beings may constitute the most difficult obstacle in the adjustment process. Therefore it would seem that in this connexion the temperamental factor has a special importance for the school. It is often debated as to whether the aim of education is primarily individual or social. An understanding of the rôle of temperament would probably help to destroy this antithesis.

It may then be not unprofitable to consider some of the theories of temperament which we have studied and try to find traces of their application in educational theory and practice. In such an attempt each theory will be considered by itself and without reference to the concluding line of investigation outlined in the last chapter, towards which, as it appears to the author, the precise study of the temperamental factor is tending.

There is one preliminary point of passing interest which may be made. As in the case of all systems whether of philosophy or of art so any formulation of educational theory may to a great extent be regarded as the temperamental expression of its exponent. It is significant that of the examples

of the great temperamental types cited by Richerand
in his treatise, two at least, Rousseau and Montaigne,
have written essays on education, and if the analysis
of their temperaments as given by Richerand
was reliable, it should help greatly towards the
understanding of their doctrines. It is doubtful
however whether the writer himself would allow
that his temperament was entitled to consideration in the appraisement of his work, since he
would rather claim that he had eliminated the
temperamental factor. In this connexion Jung
quotes the words of Wm. James. 'The History
of philosophy is to a large extent that of a clash
of human temperaments. Of whatever temperament a philosopher is he tries when he philosophizes
to sink the fact of his temperament. Yet his
temperament really gives him a stronger bias than
any of his more objective premises. Yet in the forum
he can make no claim on the bare ground of his temperament to superior discernment or authority.'[1]

But this criticism is of universal application
and need not detain us further.

The classical doctrine of the four temperaments
was held for nearly two thousand years. Its
influence should therefore be traceable in some at
least of the works of the great educational theorists
who wrote before its influence had begun to decline
or its validity to be discredited.

'In the theory of education,' says Brett, 'there
are obvious traces of the mediaeval doctrine of
humours. The physiologist tended to make the

---

[1] Quoted. Psychological Types, page 372, from Wm.
James. Pragmatism, page 7.

nature of men wholly dependent on the mixture
of elements and described each temperament as
due to the excess of one element over the others.
Plato says that man is also a mixture of natures
and a science of temperament requires as its com-
plement a science of character. Character depends
largely on the extent to which one or other of the
natures is developed. A man may be characterized
by excess of spirit or of intellect. The right proportion is that which permits of the rule of intellect
which therefore involves a theory of conduct.'[1]

It is as we have seen in the attempt to erect
on the doctrine of the temperaments a science of
character that the resultant confusion as to the
nature and limitations of the temperament has
ensued. The idea of character has overshadowed
it in importance and the development of educational
theory has been marked by a continuous merging
of the purely physical temperament, but wherever in
the writings of the educational thinkers from the
time of Plato, through the Renaissance period up
to the eighteenth century, emphasis is laid on the
disposition of the child, it is evident that the idea
of a mixture of physical elements has its place.
The 'disposition' however as cited by these writers
included all that to-day would be included in such
terms as 'temperament,' 'tendencies,' and 'capacities,' and it was inevitable that, from the angle of
their outlook, they should emphasize chiefly that
aspect which was connected with the child's
individual aptitude for specific subjects.

---

[1]History of Psychology. Vol. I., page 94.

So Erasmus writes 'It is not I believe a vain
thing to try and infer from the face and bearing
of a boy what disposition he will show. Nature
has not omitted to give us marks for our guidance
in that respect. Aristotle wrote a work on physiognomy and Virgil bids us recognise the differences
which distinguish one type of cattle from another
in regard to the uses to which we may put them.
However I am personally of the opinion that where
the method is sound, where teaching and practice
go hand in hand, any discipline may ordinarily
be acquired by the flexible intellect.'[1]

Again Vives lays down that 'Variations of mind
arise from the different nature of each person, that
is of the constitution and temperament of their
bodies—Those persons do not change whose bodily
constitution is in harmony with each stage of their
course of life. Morals also change the natural
disposition in many ways for the constitution of
the body has a great influence on the strength of
the mind and it is from the body that the passions
take their rise. Food should be varied to suit the
constitution of every individual so that no noxious
humour may strike its roots in the body. Weak
blooded people may take fluids, phlegmatic people
what is warm and healing, melancholy people
what is opposite to their nature and will make
them more gay.'[2]

The teaching of Locke, with its emphasis, on the
'blank white paper' of the child's mind, upon which
the educator could write at will, yet took account

---

[1] De pueris instituendis, 16-499ᵉ.
[2] De tradendis disciplinis. Ch. III., and IV.

of an innate ' disposition' which could not be ignored. 'Native propensities' he writes, 'will not be cured by rules—the bias will always be on the side where nature placed it. If you carefully observe the characters of his mind now in the first scenes of his life you will ever after be able to judge which way his thoughts lean. '[1] There is here no direct reference to the connexion of physical appearance and corresponding mental traits.

With the writings of Rousseau the 'disposition' of the child began to assume definitely its connexion with instinctive tendencies as they are recognised in the psychology of to-day. His insistence throughout the '*Emile*' of the close connexion between the health of the body and the vigour of the mind may perhaps be not uninfluenced by the classical doctrine of temperaments.

He says for example ' *L'inaction, la contrainte où l'on retient les membres d'un enfant, ne peuvent que gêner la circulation du sang, des humeurs, empêcher l'enfant de se fortifier, de croître et altérer sa constitution. Une contrainte si cruelle pourrait-elle ne pas influer sur leur humeur ainsi que sur leur tempérament ?*'[1] He alludes frequently in the '*Emile*' to the temperament as something essentially physical but his preoccupation is obviously with the different tendencies which manifest themselves spontaneously at the different periods of the child's development and which have their origin in the primary uniform passion of ' *amour de soi-même.*' It was the investigation of these

---

[1] Thoughts concerning Education, page 102.
[1] Emile (Edition Meynot) Book I., page 20.

tendencies which from the time of Rousseau formed the chief content of the movement for child study which he inaugurated.

The teacher of to-day frequently alludes to individual children under his care as volatile, passionate, lethargic, or highly strung. If, instead, he used the terms sanguine, choleric, phlegmatic or nervous it is conceivable that the meaning he wishes to convey would be unchanged. He may also at times imply that from the particular colouring or physical build of a child it is easy to infer the traits corresponding to the terms he uses. He would however never claim that such a ruling was anything but highly general and even superficial in character. If he wished to diagnose the type of child with a view to his individual treatment he would find it necessary to subject any such general classification to a rigorous analysis. He would also contend with obvious justification that the greater proportion of the children in his charge could not be included with any degree of accuracy under such a system of classification.

It is perhaps rather to the modern experimental attack on the temperamental problem that the teacher would be inclined to turn for precise assistance. It will be remembered that the investigations of Ach emphasized strength of determining tendencies and degree of sensitivity.

The teacher will naturally feel that he is perhaps more able to influence the strength of determining tendencies so far as this is acquired than to modify the degree of sensitiveness. Ach's suggestion that one mark of successful volitional action lies in the amount of resistance overcome has a direct educational corollary, since the resistance to be overcome can to a great extent be controlled by the educator. It is in his power to give direction to the determining tendencies and to provide for such a graduation of resistance that, on the one hand the pupil shall feel that degree of satisfaction which will be the surest means of fixing the determining tendencies, and on the other, shall provide the stimulus for a fruitful energetic decision. It may perhaps be said that of the types delineated the melancholic is most in need of this feeling of satisfaction, and that therefore, in the initial stages of an enterprise, the resistance should be reduced to a minimum while in the case of the sanguine temperament the degree of resistance should be subjected to a continuous increase. As far as is possible the conditions must be such as to maintain the energetic decision and the output of productive work.

Looked at from this aspect the question of supplementing or modifying the temperament is clearly only part of the much wider and more controversial question of the possible training of the will. It will therefore have to be connected up with the whole question of the integration of the organism, which must always form the distinctive mark of volitional action. The medium of this integration is held to be the growth of the self-regarding sentiment and all that this involves.

The training of the will would therefore become the fostering of sentiments in which the force of the organism is expressed. 'There can be no

" training of the will " apart from the general
process by which the sentiments are built up.'[1]
Such sentiments might be held to supply the energy
of the determining tendencies and would prove
the most valuable factor in maintaining its level
of persistence. To pursue such a line of thought
involves us in the consideration of those questions
of volition and perseveration the complexity of
which has been indicated in earlier chapters.
Awaiting further elucidation of these admittedly
difficult points the teacher may yet find in such
suggestions as the graduation of resistance and
organization of determining tendencies a helpful
line of approach to the practical handling of
individual differences.

The basic idea of Jung's differentiation of types
makes a strong appeal to the teacher's mind.
The distinction between inward and outward is
one with which he is familiar in his task of building
up interests and of directing activities. If, following
the advice of Froebel he strives to make the 'inner
outer, and the outer inner,' then he must feel that
if the child has an innate tendency of direction
towards the inner or the outer it is of extreme
significance. His attempt to combine the two
into an harmoniously functioning unity might be
interpreted as an effort towards the effective
dilution of types. What would however be perhaps
the chief function of the teacher would be to see
that the 'inferior function' working in the unconscious is in effect a compensatory function, not

[1]Education, its Data and First Principles (T. P. Nunn),
page 174.

an element working destructively towards a subsequent neurosis.

At first sight it might appear that the markedly extroverted type of child is the one which the average observer would be inclined to consider the more normally healthy and he would probably feel that the greater share of the teacher's assistance is required by the apparently more difficult introverted type. Jung, in his analysis lays emphasis on the fact that each of his eight types is distinguished by its own peculiar values and dangers and that these are generally found to be in direct proportion. He admits the extreme difficulty of singling out the types from external signs alone. Moreover in his description the signs considered are in many cases those which could only be looked for in mature adults. There are however certain features of some of the types which must be familiar to the observers of children or of adolescents.

Thus for example the tendency to be swallowed up in the individual feeling processes which Jung describes as the work of the extroverted feeling type is often recognizable in the early stages of adolescence. Or, again, the tendency of the introverted sensation type to wrap up the image of the sensation in a derived lustre calls up the problems of day dreams and phantasies, and the type of child in which these problems reach their most acute presentation.

A conspicuously good adjustment is given by Jung as one of the characteristics of the extroverted sensation type. Such an adjustment would naturally be received gladly as an evidence of healthy normality in a child but the limitations which accompany it in this type would serve as a warning against accepting it without an attempt to examine the security of the foundation on which it rests. In regard to the 'thinking function' it is perhaps most difficult to discover in the immature mind the particular direction towards which it is tending. The intuitive extrovert on the other hand, with his marked influence over others is familiar in the outstanding personalities of the class, while in the case of the most difficult but extremely valuable intuitive introvert the age of adolescence would appear to be the critical moment for the transference of the 'energic potential' to the moral sphere which in the opinion of Jung, may be accomplished with little disturbance.

When Miss Downey considers her results from the educational angle it is evident that her suggestions in this direction will have equal value if and when a standard classification of temperament is ultimately evolved. One of her suggestions is that teachers of different temperamental types should be selected to handle children of corresponding Will-profiles with a view to more harmonious co-operation. A question may here arise as to whether it may not be found that successful teachers tend to possess a more or less similar Will-profile, so that it will not be easy to supply each of the wide range of Will-profiles which may reasonably be expected to occur in an ordinary group of children with its educator counterpart.

The troubles of discipline may, Miss Downey points out, often be traced to the combination of high motor impulsion and low inhibition. The province of the teacher is then so to control the situations which call out motor reactions until specific habits have been acquired. This generalized statement may not seem to provide a very hopeful formula for the practical handling of such difficulties when they occur, but an understanding of the nature of the problem in hand will obviously be wholly an advantage.

In the examples we have reviewed the prime concern was with theories of temperament and the educational application was a mere corollary. We might now reverse the procedure and turning to the theories which are primarily educational try to find there the place allotted to temperament.

We have seen that of all the terms with which the temperament has been connected by modern writers, the one which most recommends itself to educational theory is given in the concept of 'Personality.' The mere coupling of temperament and personality does not elucidate the nature of either but it serves to emphasize the essentially subjective nature of each. In the chapter on 'The data of Education' in 'The Evolution of Educational Theory' Professor John Adams alludes to personality as 'almost a datum but still leaving a certain scope for the educator.' In the same chapter he discusses the rôle of temperament and whether it must be considered as a datum or as part of the field of the educator. 'The popular view' he says 'seems to be that the temperament is something not altogether within our control, and therefore something to be accepted as a datum rather than to be worked up in connexion with educational process.'[1]

Dealing with the physical aspect of temperament and pointing out its admitted susceptibility to the influence of drugs he dismisses this application as unwholesome. 'All this is too unwholesome as a basis for practical suggestion but when it comes to the influence of ordinary food stuffs we are on safer ground. Here it is admitted that a complete change of diet once established and then continued for a long period does result in certain changes. Since education has to include the physical as well as the spiritual, it is to this extent bound to take into account considerations of dietary in relation to temperament in general ; but it need not expect to do much character building by the help of a regimented dietary. The temperament may be affected generally but it is difficult to believe that much can be done in the way of producing specific changes by means of safe foodstuffs.'[2]

The question then arises 'Is this to be the end of the rôle of temperament in education that it must be modified as desirable by judicious diet ?' This is precisely the standpoint of Hippocrates. Supposing this to be accepted as a working basis, and assuming that a carefully graduated diet had been evolved we should expect from such regulation that in time children and perhaps races might become less warlike, perhaps less sluggish, and perhaps less easily excited, according to the direction in which the corrective diet was administered.

---

[1]Evolution of Educational Theory, page 43.
[2]Ibid., page 41.

That is to say such modification would make essentially for greater uniformity and would therefore tend to deprive the temperament of its primary rôle as a differentiating agent.

But according to the endocrine doctrine as outlined by Dr. Berman, the possibilities of modification by the art of the physician are by no means so limited in extent. The claim which he makes that 'the internal secretion formula of an individual may in the future constitute his measurement which will place him accurately in the social scale'[1] is not intended to imply that this formula is invariable. He lays great emphasis on the importance of the first few years of the child's life in regard to the influence which the functioning of the endocrine glands at this period is destined to have on the later development of the child. It may be argued that from every point of view educational thought lays emphasis on these early years, but in the specific nature of the formative effect which he ascribes to them Dr. Berman seems to approach the Freudian standpoint. For example he says : 'Each time the babe reacts to a pleasant or unpleasant stimulus there is an outpouring of certain internal secretions, a tingling of certain vegetative nerves and organs, a hushing of others. The ensemble of reactions tends to be repeated around the same stimulus until the whole becomes automatic. Soon comes conflict between the automatic pleasant reflex and associated reflexes formed round father, mother, etc., and so consciousness of

---

[1] The glands regulating Personality, page 23.

N

self as active wisher and of punishable suppression.'[1]

Frequently he expresses himself in what have come to be regarded as psycho-analytic terms and his conclusion may be summarised as follows :—

'Behind the instinct is now conceived the psychic wish or libido charged with Psychic Energy. The source of the psychic energy of the wish is the vegetative system. The wish is a function of the pressure and therefore a function of the concentration of substance behind pressure.'[2]

The hopes which Dr. Berman holds out of the final understanding of his types of personality and their ultimate control may be quoted in his own words :—

'Towards the process of adjustment and adaptation of the environment to the individual as well as of the individual to the environment, attitude will change from hopeless acquiescence in the inevitable to a complete self-determination of the self and its surroundings. The adventures of the personality, strung along as the episodes of his career, his friendships and sex reactions, his mishaps and diseases, and the final fate or future that overtakes him begin to be comprehensible and hence controllable.

'The crying need is for an international institute endowed and equipped for investigation. Such an institute would possess the right chemical laboratories for the making of blood analyses— metabolism examinations and tests of endocrine

---

[1] Glands regulating Personality, page 144.
[2] Ibid page 172 et seq.

functions. There would be X-ray machines and experts to radiograph the pituitary, pineal, and thymus glands where possible. There would be psychologists to carry out intelligence tests, determine emotional reactions and group mental aberrations and deficiences. It will be above all in the understanding of children—their make up, reactions, and powers that the biologist will achieve some of his finest triumphs.

'The educator will have to take account of the state of the pituitary in estimating normal intelligence. As well will he have to consider the thyroid —the child whose conduct is refractory even though his proficiency in his studies is excellent. And the condition of the adrenal will be ascertained in the types that tire easily and that seem unable to make the effort necessary or desirable. Periodic seasonal and critical fluctuations in the equilibrium among the hormones will have to be taken into account in the explanation of what has hitherto been put down to laziness, naughtiness, stupidity or obstinacy. No science was possible in the matter of classification for variation without the insight into the physiology of the candidate that the analysis of the endocrine will provide.

'How much are we to tolerate of malignant abnormality and disregard benign abnormality altogether for the sake of the valuable that is concomitant ? '

'It is safe to predict that it is now somewhat possible and will become more possible to regulate and even check the ills of genius without interfering with its highest evolution and expression.

'The right of the power to modify like the power to kill will be defined and limited by common agreement.'[1]

In the present incomplete state of knowledge, we must perhaps distrust the ease with which Dr. Berman forges the transition link between physiological processes and such factors as the 'psychic wish.' To his hopes of regulation of conduct by the processes of injection we may at least listen with appreciation. We may be inclined to consider the picture which he draws as picturesque rather than scientific but the line of argument followed in the earlier chapters of this book points, as we have seen, to an increasing recognition of the extreme importance of the endocrine glands in their influence on behaviour. It will be remembered that Dr. McDougall mentions that of the physical components of temperament the ductless glands are undoubtedly the most important.

'To some minds the contemplation of the facts of this order is profoundly disturbing. Others complacently look forward to the time when further knowledge of them may enable us to intervene in the processes of development, to improve upon the work of Nature. But the facts are of profound importance and must be faced and taken fully into account by the psychologist.'[2]

If they have this profound importance for the psychologist it follows automatically that for the educator they will have an equal significance.

A hint of the possibility of modification of the endocrine secretions, other than by physical means

---

[1] Glands regulating Personality, pages 230-253.
[2] Outline of Psychology, page 356.

is given in the article already referred to, published by Dr. Leonard Williams in the British Journal of Psychology for July 1922. 'That education is merely a process partly of organized and purposeful suggestion, and largely of suggestion which is purely fortuitous and haphazard must be obvious to anyone who will give the matter a moment's serious consideration. This factor of suggestion is one of enormous importance in the eventual determination of the endocrine pattern, for the various glands of the system will have to adapt themselves to the surrounding suggestional atmosphere and when they fail to do so trouble arises. Psychologists talk a good deal about failure in adaptation but not very many of them realize that the difficulties are primarily and fundamentally of endocrine origin. When the glandular cause of such conflicts comes to be generally recognized their treatment by psychical methods will be rendered very much more simple and satisfactory by reinforcing it with remedial measures applied to the glands themselves.'

At the present stage of development of the endocrine doctrine it is impossible to estimate the precise effects which its elaboration may produce on educational practice. It is perhaps possible to say that, assuming the laboratory manipulation of the glands to have reached the stage of perfection shadowed by Dr. Berman, the chief importance for the educator will lie in the classification rather than in the modification of personality. Such classifications will take their place side by side with Intelligence Tests in assessing the educability of the individual. They will also provide a valuable key to the treatment of the child from the point of view of educational method. In this connection it follows at once that they will strengthen the case for individual rather than for class teaching.

As to the possibility of influencing glandular secretions by suggestion and of so controlling the subsequent manifestation in behaviour it is clear that the teacher would gladly welcome a scientifically worked out technique which would accomplish this desirable result. We are reminded at this point of the conviction expressed by Watson that the activity of the endocrine glands is subject to the process of conditioning.

Laboratory tests of temperament, with a view to its classification, have already been attempted on bases other than that of the endocrine glands. Their basis has been either that of emotional reaction or of 'the varying directions taken by our spontaneous processes of thought.' Account is taken of these by the recently published report of the Board of Education on 'Psychological Tests of Educable Capacity.' Examples of tests undertaken with the aim of evolving a measurement of temperament as an aspect of personality distinct from the concept of character are seen in the American investigations already quoted. The report of the Consultative Committee concludes as we noted above that experimental machinery for the testing of temperament is at present so imperfect that the method of observation must still be considered the most important instrument for this purpose. The importance of an estimate of temperament both from the points of view of vocational guidance and educational treatment is fully realised, and the urgency for the development of experimental investigation along these lines is emphasized.

'When all is said, the problems of temperament and character still constitute one of the most difficult and urgent provinces for future psychological research.' (Report of the Consultative Committee on Psychological Test of Educable Capacity, Ch.I., Section XIV.).

In commenting upon the nature of the results which the laboratory manipulation of temperament may be expected to yield, it may be permissible to express the hope that such treatment may eventually lead to the correction by the organism itself of its temperamental handicap. While for example, the disciplinary difficulties which may be expected to arise in the child of excessive thyroid activity may be resolved to his clear advantage by corrective injections, a still greater advantage will undoubtedly accrue to him when conditions can be so controlled for him that his own organism can itself regulate the quantitative functioning of his glands. It may be that the clue to such self-regulation is to be found in suggestion as outlined above.

We might proceed to consider the possibility of influence by suggestion in conjunction with the problem of the 'unconscious mind' as it is stated by the Psycho Analytic School of Thought, but this would lead us far away from the narrower problem of 'temperament.' In Chapter VIII we endeavoured to link up to some extent the theses of Freud and Jung with the available knowledge of the working of the endocrine glands. The teacher is quick to appreciate the help which he derives from the study of the theories and methods of Psycho-Analysis and of Analytical Psychology. Should the concept of temperament eventually be narrowed down on the lines which we have indicated, or even eliminated altogether, the contribution of these two schools of thought to educational practice will remain untouched.

Meanwhile failing a standardized connotation of the term 'temperament' it is perhaps open to the practical teacher to formulate for himself a concept which shall at least have meaning for his work. If he is unwilling to accept it merely as a datum, he must either look elsewhere for its physical modification or bring to bear upon it his own power of suggestion. This will at the best be that of an efficient amateur unless he lays down for himself clear limits to his field of action. For this purpose he is entitled to seize upon any aspects of temperament which may seem to him to give clarity to his own conception. At the moment the first consideration seems to be, that at least until it is standardised, the classification of temperament is of less importance than its function.

If, and when a satisfactory classification of temperament is arrived at, its value to the educator will be two-fold. In the first place it will influence any system of grading. Since the object of grading is the adjustment of the matter and method of instruction to the characteristics of the grade, the classification of temperaments will have an immediate effect upon the methods employed by the educator in individual cases.

In the second case it will supply a basis for interpolation. Knowing the temperament graph of the pupil, the educator can in theory predict what will be the nature of the response in given conditions. Therefore, either it is open to him to modify the conditions in order to obtain the required response, or keeping the conditions constant to use the particular response as the basis of further work.

While therefore, with a standard classification of temperament it would be possible for the teacher to say: 'Since the child has such and such a temperament, therefore to such conditions he will respond in such a way,' as it is, failing such a classification, all that he can apparently do is to recognize the work of temperament when he sees its results in the child's reactions. To say in such a connexion : 'This is the work of temperament' is equivalent to admitting that on these grounds it must be accorded an individual treatment. The value of an increased knowledge will not be in the formulation of a few additional maxims of treatment but in the adaptation which each teacher will evolve for himself from his knowledge of the children in his charge.

If the temperament is eventually regarded as a general factor influencing behaviour, then on the emotional side its effect may have to be considered as that of a general affective tone, colouring all activities. If, following the view of Shand, it is argued that only the 'temper' of specific emotions can be described, then the educator will be concerned only with its effects on the formation of specific sentiments. His observations of each child from the temperamental point of view will then tend to be detailed and discrete.

The popular view which ascribes the particular colouring of the emotional relations of people one to another as the work of temperament is confirmed by scientific observation of the child's development. The psycho-analytic school in particular emphasize the most intimate connexion which exists between the mental development of the child and his emotional relations with the members of his own family. Dr. H. von Hug-Hellmuth for example in her monograph on 'A study of the Mental Life of the Child' says specifically 'The first definite signs of his being attracted towards other people come into existence along the path of his intellectual development.

'The development of the rational powers proceeds not at the expense of emotional life but hand in hand with it.'[1]

The removal of repressions by the practice of Psycho-Analysis, and the assistance in the sublimation of instincts which is ascribed as the peculiar field of the educator can no doubt dissolve the graver conflicts of personal relationships. It is unlikely that they can remove the temperamental bias which colours all personal relationships in however slight a degree. It can be well argued that such colouring is not in itself a defect to be deplored, but rather an added interest to be understood. The same individual differences may

---

[1] Study of the Mental Life of the Child, page 25.

be the source of interest or of irritation according as they are understood and appreciated or attacked in ignorance. It is continually being urged that children at school should be helped to appreciation of beauty in the sphere of art, to appreciation of character in the figures of history, and to respect for the rights of others in the ordinary routine of life. To this it might be added that through art, history, manners or morality, they might be helped towards an appreciation of those finer emotional shades of personality, which failing a more precise definition are ascribed to the temperamental factor.

Conversation is still considered worthy to be called a fine art, although it has no academic or professional claims, and in this category also might perhaps be placed the appreciation of temperamental differences.

In conclusion it may be urged that while the attempt we have made in the preceding chapters to narrow the conception of temperament may appear to detract from the picturesque and somewhat apologetic significance which it conveys in common usage, such delimitation, if established, would help to provide for the teacher a finer and more delicate instrument for successful contact with the children in his charge.

BIBLIOGRAPHY

ADAMS, J. Evolution of Educational Theory . . 1912
BERMAN, L. The Glands Regulating Personality . 1921
BRETT, G. S. History of Psychology, Vol. I. . 1912–21
BROCK, A. J. Galen on the Natural Faculties . . 1916
BURTON, R. Anatomy of Melancholy 1621
    Bohn's Edition 1923
CANNON, W. Bodily Changes in Pain, Hunger, Fear
    and Rage 1920
DOWNEY, J. The Will Temperament and its Testing . 1923
ERASMUS. De Pueris Instituendis (Woodward's Trans-
    lation) 1529
FOUILLÉE, A. Tempérament et Caractère . . . 1895
GALEN. Works of Galen (French Translation by Charles
    Darenberg). Translation, 1854 . . . 200 A.D.
HIPPOCRATES. Air, Water and Places. Translated by
    W. H. S. Jones. Translation, 1923 . . 400 B.C.
HOCH AND AMSDEN. Descriptive Study of Personality
    (Review of Neurology and Psychiatry) . Nov. 1913
HUG-HELLMUTH. Study of Mental Life of the Child . 1919
JORDAN-FURNEAUX. Anatomy and Physiology . . 1890
JUNG, C. J. Psychological Types 1923
LANKES, W. Perseveration (British Journal of Psycho-
    logy) 1915
LOCKE, J. Thoughts concerning Education . . . 1693
MCDOUGALL, W. Outline of Psychology . . . 1923
MAHER, M. Test Book of Psychology (7th Edition) . 1911
MILLER, E. Types of Mind and Body 1926
MOON, R. O. Hippocrates and his Successors . . 1923
NUNN, T. P. Education—its Data and First Principles 1920
RICHERAND. Physiology. Translation by G. D. M.
    de Lys 1812
ROBACK, A. A. Psychology of Character . . . 1927
ROUSSEAU, J. J. Emile 1762
SHAND, A. F. Foundations of Character . . . 1914
STEWART, A. Our Temperaments 1892
VIVES. De Tradendis Disciplinis (Translation by Foster
    Watson) 1531
WATSON, J. B. Psychology from the Standpoint of a
    Behaviourist 1924
WATSON, J. B. Behaviourism 1925
WEBB, E. Character and Intelligence (British Journal
    of Psychology—Monograph Supplement) . . 1915
WHATELY SMITH, W. The Measurement of Emotion . 1922
WILLIAMS, L. The Constituents of the Unconscious
    (British Journal of Psychology—Medical Section)
                                July, 1922

INDEX

Printed in Great Britain by
Wyman & Sons, Ltd , London, Fakenham and Reading.

For Product Safety Concerns and Information please contact our EU
representative GPSR@taylorandfrancis.com
Taylor & Francis Verlag GmbH, Kaufingerstraße 24, 80331 München, Germany

* 9 7 8 0 3 6 7 4 1 8 5 1 9 *